CUBA

The Legend of Rum

CUBA
The Legend of Rum

WRITTEN BY

ANISTATIA MILLER, JARED BROWN,
WITH
DAVE BROOM & NICK STRANGEWAY

HAVANA CLUB COLLECTION
MIXELLANY BOOKS

All correspondence should be addressed to the publisher's attention at: Mixellany, 13 Bonchurch Road, London W13 9JE United Kingdom.

Photo Credits:
Exposition Universelle des Vins et Spiritueux: 58
Havana Club Collection: 2, 6, 22, 50, 68, 69, 70, 73, 75, 76, 81, 82, 85, 86, 87, 88, 91, 92, 94, 96, 98, 100, 102, 104, 106, 108, 110, 117, 119, 125, 133, 137, 149, 155, 158, 161, 173, 177
Jared Brown and Anistatia Miller, personal collection: 10, 27, 35, 36, 37, 49, 53, 56, 64, 110, 111, 112, 114, 120, 122, 125, 128, 129, 130, 139, 141, 145, 158, 159, 160
Public domain: 12, 48, 55, 61, 65, 157, 166, 169, 170, 171
Corbis: 15, 18
New York Public Library Digital Galleries: 16, 21, 24, 29, 31, 33, 34, 39, 40, 42, 44, 165

Designed by Mixellany

First edition
ISBN: 0-9760937-8-2

10 9 8 7 6 5 4 3 2

This book, part of the Havana Club Collection, is
dedicated to Fernando Campoamor—Cuban journalist
and author, confidant of novelist Ernest Hemingway and
one of the finest historians on the subject of Cuban rum.

ABOVE:
This model of an old-style
continuous still used for making
rum is located at Havana Club's
Museo del Ron in Old Havana.

Preface

THE HISTORIES OF SUGARCANE and its ethereal descendant—authentic Cuban rum—are closely associated with the legends of the Cuban nation, with its countryside, its culture, its music and its spirit. In this book you will discover the true roots of Cuban rum: from its relationships with people from explorer Christopher Columbus to author Ernest Hemingway; with places from the aging cellars at the distilleries to the legendary bars of Havana; and with its multicultural influences that they transformed into a distinctive Cuban identity; and with the embodiment of that persona in art, in literature, in music, in spirituality and in life itself.

The original book *Cuba: Legend of Rum* was published in 1996 by Editions Bahia Presse under the editorial direction of Jean Baudot. Some elements of it have been integrated in this newly revised edition.

This is a tale of passion and imagery, in which kings and conquistadors, pirates and planters, master rum blenders and bartenders, international movie stars and industrial magnates, revolutionaries and romanticists each play a significant role.

Fernando G. Campoamor once quoted an assessment of Cuban rum written in 1925: "In truth, there never has been and never will be rum as good as ours. Those made outside Cuba lack the best raw material that exists, molasses made from Cuban sugarcane."

In this volume, the secrets of producing fine Cuban rums such as Havana Club, of tasting the celebrated *añejos* and for making some of Cuba's most famous classic cocktails are also disclosed.

The history of Cuba a wondrous legend of a land, its people and its national drink. So the journey begins.

Contents

CHAPTER ONE

The New World

COLUMBUS DISCOVERS CUBA & ITS PEOPLE

OPPOSITE:
The eastern portion of the long,
narrow island of Cuba was the
first point of discovery from
explorers such as Christopher
Columbus when they first
encountered the New World.

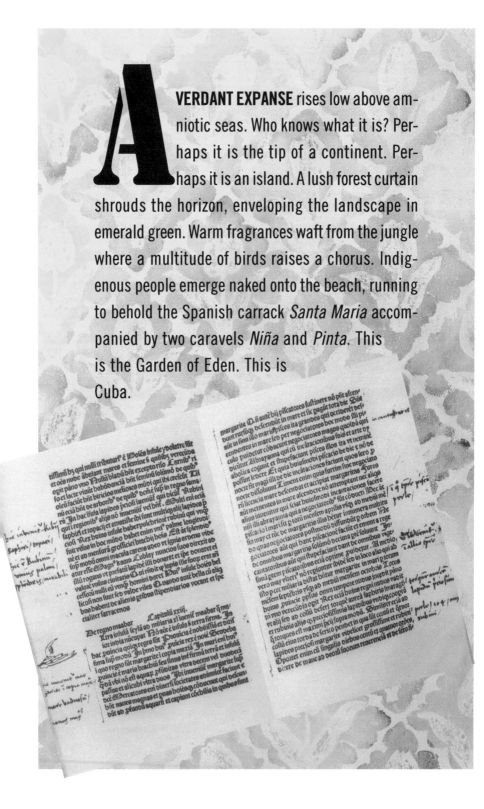

A **VERDANT EXPANSE** rises low above amniotic seas. Who knows what it is? Perhaps it is the tip of a continent. Perhaps it is an island. A lush forest curtain shrouds the horizon, enveloping the landscape in emerald green. Warm fragrances waft from the jungle where a multitude of birds raises a chorus. Indigenous people emerge naked onto the beach, running to behold the Spanish carrack *Santa Maria* accompanied by two caravels *Niña* and *Pinta*. This is the Garden of Eden. This is Cuba.

IT IS SUNDAY, 28 October 1492. Explorer Christopher Columbus is bedazzled by this paradise. He writes in his journal: "This is the most beautiful land the eyes of man have ever looked upon."

Columbus is convinced that this newly discovered land is the eastern frontier of the mighty empire of the Great Khan of Cathay. No one on board this fleet knows that an enormous continent—a new world—separates the Orient from the Atlantic. No one guesses this landfall is the largest island in an archipelago of more than 4,000 islands and keys strung loosely at the edge of the Tropic of Cancer near the mouth of the Gulf of Mexico. In a few years, Europeans will call this region the Caribbean, the Antilles, the West Indies.

First Encounters

BUT NO, THIS NEW TERRITORY was not Cipango, as Columbus first believed. Cipango, a poetic name used by the thirteenth-century Venetian traveller Marco Polo to describe the island empire of Japan. In his memoir *Il Millione,* which he dictated to Rustichello of Pisa in 1298, Polo recounted that in Cipango:

> *...the quantity of gold they have is endless; for they find it in their own Islands and the King does not*

OPPOSITE:
A reenactment of
Christopher Columbus
taking possession, in
1492, of the Caribbean
island of San Salvador.

allow it to be exported. Moreover few merchants visit the country because it is so far from the main land and thus it comes to pass that their gold is abundant beyond all measure."

And when Don Cristóbal, on a sea of indigo,
Saw rise and grow that island of his ecstasy,
A hundred pilots, sharing in this fantasy,
Dropped Iberian anchors in the ports of Cipango.

Gold, above all else, was the element that lured European monarchs to cast their attentions toward the exotic kingdoms of the Orient, sending emissaries across the Silk Routes by land and by sea. Gold was the reason King Ferdinand II of Aragon and Queen Isabella I of Castile commissioned Columbus to seek a new and faster passage to the Orient by sailing to the west.

Upon reaching San Salvador—in what is now The Bahamas—Columbus and his crew heard tales about a neighboring land to the west that led him to believe he had succeeded in his quest:

> *I have heard these people say that it [Cuba] was very large and of great traffic and that there were in it gold and spices and great ships and merchants.*

Sea Quadrant

An Instrument containing y.e 4.th part of a Circle, or 90 deg; well con trived for y.e Mariner's use, y.e great Arch plac't at a Convenient distance for y.e Eye, y.e lesser for y.e Shadow.

ABOVE:
A quadrant of the type used by Columbus was an instrument that measured the altitude of celestial bodies, consisting of a 90° graduated arc with a movable radius for measuring angles.

And they showed me that I should go to it by the west-southwest and I think so. For I think that if I may trust the signs which all the Indians of these islands have made me and those whom I am carrying in the ships, for by the tongue I do not understand them, it [Cuba] is the Island of Cipango, of which wonderful things are told and on the globes which I have seen and in the painted maps, it is in this district.

The land he encountered was so vast, Columbus was convinced Cuba was the peninsula of a large continent—to his dying day. As he related in his journal:

And it is certain that this is the mainland and that I am before Zayto and Quinsay [two ports mentioned by Marco Polo], *a hundred leagues more or less from both of them and this is clearly shown by the tide, which comes in a different manner from that in which it has done up to this time; and yesterday when I went to the northwest I found that it was cold.*

The first Cubans that Columbus encountered were the peaceful, highly-civilized Taínos. They subsisted by fishing, hunting and farming yucca, maize and tobacco. They called their home *Cubanacan*, meaning "the abundantly fertile land". Fearful at the first sighting of the Spanish explorers, the Taínos were eventually fascinated. They presumed

BELOW:
Upon his return to Spain,
Christopher Columbus
presented a group of Taínos to
the Spanish Court.

these new strangers with pale skin had descended from heaven. The Ciboney and Guanahatabetes, who also inhabited Cuba, came to believe the strangers, who scoured the northern coast in search of gold, were deities adopting human form.

Taken with this bountiful island, Columbus claimed the land in the name of Spain, calling it Isla Juana, after Prince Juan of Asturias, the only son of Ferdinand and Isabella to survive to adulthood. Columbus and his crew remained in Cuba until 12 November. When they departed, they brought

ten Taíno men and women plus three children to present to Ferdinand and Isabella because:

> ...they might learn our tongue, so as to know what there is in the country and so that when they come back they may be tongues to the Christians and receive our customs and the things of the faith. Because I saw and know that this people has no religion...nor are they idolaters, but very mild and without knowing what evil is, nor how to kill others, nor how to take them and without arms and so timorous that from one of our men ten of them fly, although they do sport with them and ready to believe and knowing that there is a God in heaven and sure that we have come from heaven...

Columbus never found the endless veins of gold promised in Marco Polo's memoirs and the tales told by the natives of the new land. He did, however, realize there was potential in the planting of "white gold"—sugarcane—in the new world.

Honey Cane

COLUMBUS WAS NOT UNFAMILIAR with sugarcane. A native of Southeast Asia, the sweet grass traveled from China to India to the Near East and North Africa, becoming an important commodity for Arab, Venetian and Genoese merchants. Its unrivaled sweetness tantalized Europeans as early as 320 BC, hen Alexander the Great's admiral Nearchus first tasted the cane that grew in northern India and described it as a reed which "gives honey without bees." Around 700 AD, the conquering Saracens introduced cane seedlings to the island of Sicily. Moorish invaders sowed it in Spain and Portugal. The European taste for sugar was born and spread like a weed as crusaders returned from the Near East and North Africa with this new "spice". Demand was so great by the early 1400s that Prince Henry the Navigator of Portugal introduced plantings of the sweet grass to the island of Madeira. By 1483, the Spanish had established cane plantations in the Canary Islands.

The young Columbus began his apprenticeship, in 1473, as a business agent for the Genoese Centurione, Di Negro and Spinola trading families. One of the families' most lucrative commodities was sugar. Traveling from the Mediterranean to northern Europe, he learned the trading value of sugar, eventually moving to Madeira and Porto Santo. There, he married Filipa Moniz Perestrello, daughter of Porto Santo's governor Bartolomeu Perestrello, a Portuguese nobleman of Genoese origin.

Madeira was already established as a major sugar-producing center. Its plantation owners had grown rich from the islands' abundant harvests. Columbus knew from living

CHRISTOPHER COLUMBUS and his SONS DIEGO and FERDINAND.

Wilson Sculp.

there for nearly decade there was profit in planting and trading "white gold."

According to Fernando Campoamor in his landmark 1985 book *El Hijo Alegre de la Caña de Azúcar*, Columbus brought sugarcane seedlings with him on his second voyage to the Caribbean in 1493. But there is a sad footnote to this milestone. The great explorer was unable to conduct the cultivation experiments he intended to perform in Hispañola. The delicate plants did not survive the sea crossing. It was another seven years before Pedro di Atienza successfully imported and planted sugarcane seedlings on Hispañola. It was then that the early settlers discovered sugarcane could flourish in the tropical Caribbean climate.

OPPOSITE: A species of sugarcane eventually called Creole was originally imported from the Canary Islands and Madeira to the Caribbean where it flourished.

Blood, Sweat & Macheteros

◇◇◇◇◇◇◇◇◇◇◇◇◇◇◇◇◇◇◇◇◇◇

PEACEFUL COEXISTENCE amongst the indigenous people of Cuba and the Spanish explorers was fleeting. Columbus's two visits to Cuba never developed into the establishment of a settlement. In fact, his sole quest along the Cuban coast was for a fabled land of gold he was certain existed nearby—in Japan.

Spanish settlement of Cuba came abruptly and violently in 1512, when conquistadors Diego Velásquez de

HERNAN CORTES.

ENGRAV'D BY W. CREATBACH
From a Drawing in the Collection of the late
Don Antonio Uguina of Madrid

Cuéllar and his secretary Hernán Cortés arrived with three hundred men and fresh sugarcane seedlings. They forced the Taínos to plant the shoots in the newly bared earth after clearing the lush tropical forest that had been their home. The success of this crop led Cortés to attempt sugarcane cultivation in Mexico a few years later.

By 1515, seven cities were established on Cuba: Santiago de Cuba, Bayamo, Trinidad, Havana, Baracoa, Camagüey and Sancti Spiritus. Velásquez became the island's governor, Cortés the mayor of Santiago de Cuba. Velásquez and Cortés stopped looking for gold in Cuba. Within two decades, the Spanish were certain the legendary El Dorado—the Golden Man—and his city resided in South America, where conquistadors found the palaces, gardens and people of the Inca Empire gilded in gold.

The conquistadors who remained in Cuba turned their attentions to the wealth that could be had in sugar. By 1570, the majority of the 270 Spanish families settled in Cuba had established sprawling sugar plantations and operated sugar mills. Sugar was a labor-intensive proposition. First, land needed to be cleared of lush vegetation for planting. It takes 5,000 to 8,000 seed-cane stems to produce one acre of hand-planted sugarcane. Once it matured (in about eighteen months), the *macheteros* wielded heavy machetes in the sweltering heat to cut the cane as close to the bottom as possible because the lower portion of the stalk is much higher in sucrose.

The intense stench of rotting cane consumed workers in the sugar mills as it was simpler to harvest than to process. According to Bartolomé de las Casas, colonist Miguel de Ballester and a person named Aguiló discovered that a native tool called a *cunyaya* was effective for extracting cane juice. But even this took great strength and energy to employ. The heat in the sugar mills was so intense that workers were rotated in four-hour cycles to crush the cane, to boil the juice, to skim the hot liquid, to transfer it from kettle to kettle to reduce the developing syrup into crystals, all while maintaining a fire to provide enough heat for the process.

At first the Taínos were forced into labor, housed in squalid conditions. Foreign germs such as smallpox, scarlet fever and tuberculosis killed as many or more labourers than the backbreaking work and physical abuse at the hands of the plantation and sugar mill owners.

One man stood in defense of the native Cubans, Fray Bartolomé de las Casas. The first priest to be ordained in the New World, de las Casas arrived in the Caribbean with his father in 1502. He entered the Dominican order eight years later, becoming a missionary, in 1512, to the tormented

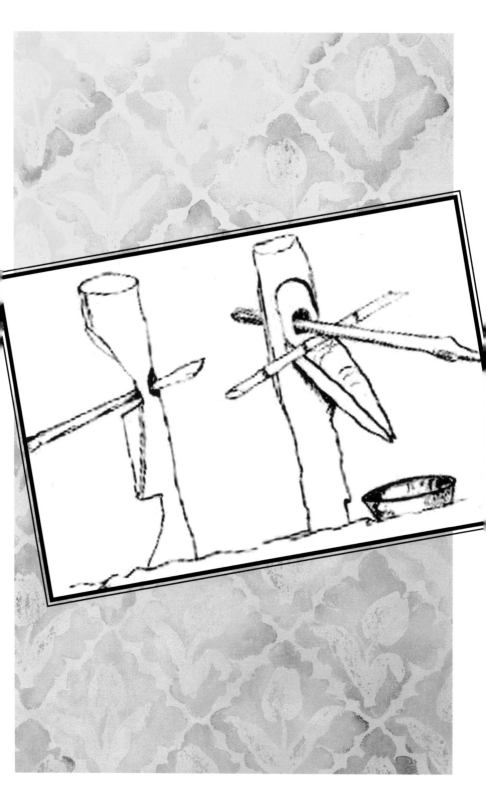

Taínos. Eyewitness to the genocide of his spiritual flock by Velàsquez's conquistadors, in 1515, de las Casas penned an impassioned letter begging King Ferdinand to end the devastation. With encouragement from Archbishop Jimenez de Cisneros of Toledo, Ferdinand appointed de las Casas Priest-procurator of the Indies, protector of the Taínos.

But the genocide did not diminish. De las Casas returned to Spain four years later to plead his case once again, this time before King Charles I. His mission met with failure. Unable to gain political support he wrote an inflammatory account of the atrocities in 1523, which became the basis for his 1542 book *A Brief Account of the Destruction of the Indies: Or, a faithful NARRATIVE OF THE Horrid and Unexampled Massacres, Butcheries and all manner of Cruelties, that Hell and Malice could invent, committed by the Popish Spanish Party on the inhabitants of West-India, TOGETHER With the Devastations of several Kingdoms in America by Fire and Sword, for the space of Forty and Two Years, from the time of its first Discovery by them.*

> *The Spaniards first assaulted the innocent Sheep, so qualified by the Almighty, as is premention'd, like most cruel Tygers, Wolves and Lions hunger-starv'd, studying nothing, for the space of Forty Years, after their first landing, but the Massacre of these Wretches, whom they have so inhumanely and barbarously butcher'd and harass'd with several kinds of Torments, never before known, or heard*

(of which you shall have some account in the following Discourse) that of Three Millions of Persons, which lived in Hispañola itself, there is at present but the inconsiderable remnant of scarce Three Hundred. Nay the Isle of Cuba, which extends as far, as Valledolid in Spain is distant from Rome, lies now uncultivated, like a Desert and intomb'd in its own Ruins.

De las Casas's pleas and prayers were partially answered in 1537, when Pope Paul III issued the papal bull

Sublimis Deus, which declared the indigenous people of the West Indies as rational beings with souls and that their lives and property should be protected. Five years later, the Church's stand on the subject compelled King Charles I to sign laws, which prohibited enslavement of the indigenous people. Although the first African slaves were smuggled into the Caribbean in 1514, it wasn't until these laws were set into motion—coupled with the realization of enormous profits from sugar—that the full-scale slave trade began in the Caribbean.

There is a chain of events that few historians properly report on this subject. The slave trade existed within Africa and the East Indies since the 1100s, primarily instigated by West African kings. Tribesmen from Central and South African territories and kingdoms were captured and sold by Angolan and Ivory Coast chiefs who had an affinity for *akpeteshi* or *burukutu* [date-palm wine], which was not dissimilar to the sugar-cane arrack exported by traders from India, Indonesia and Malaysia. Often, those enslaved were unwanted rivals for territory and resources kidnapped or hunted down and shipped to parts unknown.

This societal framework played facilitated the development of the international slave trade during the next century as colonists in Brazil and the Caribbean made lucrative

ROI D'ANGOLA.

Paris chez Duflos rue St Victor.   Tiré de l'Histoire des Voyages.   A.P.D.R.

deals with these kings. Date-palm wine and similar fermented beverages (not distilled spirits) were integral to West African culture and ritual. Consequently, rum, rhum and cachaça (sold as *jeretiba*) were quickly recognized as more powerful versions of a favoured commodity. Many economists cite this international exchange of distilled spirits for human cargo as the birth of capitalism and the global economy.

During its first century, the sugar industry in the Caribbean rapidly grew. By 1620, Cuba alone had some fifty full-scale sugar mills. But then the pace came to nearly a standstill.

OPPOSITE:
Captured by tribal chiefs and sold into slavery throughout the Caribbean, tribespeople from Central and South Africa were forced into labor amid the growing number of sugar plantations.

CHAPTER TWO

Water of Life

THE BIRTH & DEVELOPMENT OF CUBAN RUM

OPPOSITE:
A copper pot still with retorts was
the earliest style of distillation
equipment used to make rum in
the Caribbean.

IT MUST HAVE SEEMED like the Promised Land to early European emigrants. Sapphire skies, turquoise seas, rich soil, a virgin landscape. It was a new frontier, brimming with potential. The other European powers who followed the Spanish to this cornucopia in the 1600s saw sugarcane as the source of untold riches.

THE ECONOMIC PARADISE that was Cuba was soon outstripped by sugar plantations established on Barbados, Jamaica, the French Antilles and in Brazil. With wine and beer spoiling on the long ocean voyage and brandy too expensive to import, colonists resorted to making their own alcoholic beverages. Familiar with arrack, a southeast Asian spirit made from sugarcane juice imported to Europe by Arab and Genoese merchants as far back as the Crusades, colonists began to produce their own spirit.

Inspired by the success Spanish settlers in Santiago de Tequila, Mexico had with distilling the sweet, toasted juice of the agave plant in 1531, Portuguese colonists in Brazil produced, in 1533, an *aguardente de caña* from *garapa azeda* (sugarcane wine). This particular experiment was so successful that

by 1585 Brazil had 192 established distilleries.

The Spanish settlers, such as those who were distilling molasses—the thick dark syrup produced when the cane juice is boiled down to sugar crystals—at Guayacan in 1598, named their spirit *aguardiente de caña.*

Chartered in 1621, the Dutch West India Company was largely responsible for the development of the "sugar brandy" industry throughout the Caribbean. Brazil became the world's largest sugar producer and exporter after the company captured and maintained northeastern Brazil for thirty years.

The British settled in Barbados in 1627 and the French, under orders from Cardinal Richelieu, colonized Martinique eight years later. However, the sugar and distilling industries were absent until a few years later. According to some historical sources, in 1637, Dutch émigré Pietr Blower brought cane seedlings and distillery equipment to Barbados from Brazil, encouraging the distillation of molasses to extend the value of a harvest. A traveler to the island Henry Colt noted that Barbadians were "devourers upp of hott waters [*sic*] and such good distillers thereof."

Six years later, evidence that Cuban planters also acquired the technology and equipment to produce distilled spirits. As Cuban historian Miguel Bonera uncovered

an early mention of Cuban *aguardiente de caña* distillation, dating from 1643, in which Concillor Alvaro de Luces stated in a meeting that: "in almost all the sugar mills they make *aguardiente de cachaza* and in others *aguardiente de caña* ...which they sell in their bars."

The American colonies also began loading their stills with fermented molasses. The first New England rum distillery was built in Boston in 1657, not long after the Pilgrims arrived on board the *Mayflower,* in 1620 and established the Massachusetts colony. The Dutch followed in 1664, making "brandy-wine" from molasses at the colony of New Amsterdam, which is now known as New York.

Cuba benefited most from the establishment of these northern distilleries. Here were eager consumers of molasses, a commodity that was cheaper to produce than sugar. Shipping the product was cheap because of their proximity to the Caribbean.

It was during the 1650s that the Spanish *aguardiente de caña*, the French *guildive*, the British "Kill-Devil" (likely a mis-pronunciation of the French *guildive*) were respectively renamed *ron, rhum* and rum. This way, the ruling European classes could disassociate their appreciation of this brandy replacement that was also the pleasure of pirates and peons.

There are two stories about the British expression "Kill-Devil" and the French term *guildive*. One is that the French is a mispronunciation of "Kill-Devil". The other is that *guildive* is a compound of the old French term *guiller* [to ferment (as in beer)] or *giler* [to spout out], combined with *dive* a contraction of *diable* [devil].

This wasn't the fine rum we know today. Initially it was considered only worthy to be drunk by workers and slaves. That changed as sugar planters realized that if they improved the quality of this molasses distillate, they could increase profits from the crop.

Cuban settlers, however, watched as neighboring islands grew fat on the profits from sugar. The Spanish were

The consumption of rum has long been associated with the pirates who marauded the Caribbean from the 1500s through the 1800s. This illustration by Howard Pyle depicts Captain Kidd with a bottle of rum and a grog tot for sipping it.

RUM BY ANY OTHER NAME

SPECULATION SURROUNDS THE ORIGINS of the word "rum". Some people have said it was derived from the word "rummage". But that term actually dates back to 1582 and implies that a person is making a thorough search of something or some place. Others have said the word was born from the British word "rummer"—or German *roemer*—which is a type of wine glass. But these vessels appeared in Europe at the same time as the cane-juice liquor.

One romantic suggestion holds that "rum" is an abbreviated version of "rumney", a type of wine made in Greece and the southern Balkans similar to the sweet dessert wine called mavrodaphne.

According to nineteenth-century philologist Walter William Skeat, the term is an Anglicised version of the Malay word brum, which is an arrack made from sugarcane juice. Historian Frederick H. Smith found that the first documented use of the word "rum" appears in a plantation deed recorded in Barbados in 1650, which identifies the Three Houses estate in St. Philip parish as having "four large mastick cisterns for liquor for Rum."

A year later, Barbardos resident Giles Silvester made the only known reference linking the words "rum" and "rumbullion" when he wrote: "the chiefe fudling they make in the Iland is Rumbullions, als Kill Divill, and this is made of Suggar cones distilled in a hott hellish and terrible liquor." The term "rumbullion" was a common word in Devonshire, England that means "a great tumult."

However, its birth came about, the word "rum" was adopted throughout the Caribbean in the seventeenth century. First appearing in the 1750s in Diderot and Alembert's *Encyclopedie*, the word rhum with an "h" is specifically used to describe rums made in French colonies such as Martinique and Guadeloupe. The word ron, indicates the sugarcane liquor was produced in Spanish colonies, the most famous of which is the island of Cuba.

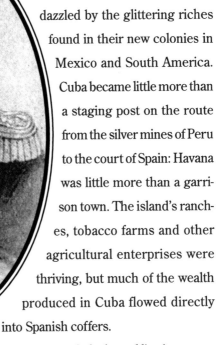

dazzled by the glittering riches found in their new colonies in Mexico and South America. Cuba became little more than a staging post on the route from the silver mines of Peru to the court of Spain: Havana was little more than a garrison town. The island's ranches, tobacco farms and other agricultural enterprises were thriving, but much of the wealth produced in Cuba flowed directly into Spanish coffers.

If the distillers of western Cuba hoped live in comparable splendor to Jamaican rum producers, they were in for a further disappointment. By the start of the eighteenth century—as rum punch was becoming a populist drink across Europe and the North American colonies—the protectionist Spanish court banned distillation in their territorial possessions to safeguard domestic wine and brandy production.

Cuban *aguardiente de caña* producers ignored the decree, but the extensive exports necessary for growth were out of the question. It wasn't until the British occupied the island for eleven months between 1762 and 1763 that they received some relief. Although the British were masters of Cuba for less than a year, the occupation signalled a change in the island's fortunes. Four thousand slaves were imported during this brief occupation, indicating the British intent to exploit Cuba's potential as a sugar colony.

Indeed, after Britain returned Cuba to Spanish control in exchange for Florida in the Treaty of Paris, the transformation continued. The ban on distilling was lifted. Havana's cane spirits were soon praised "as excellent and sweet as the island's sugar".

Revolution & Evolution

IT TOOK A REVOLUTION ON ANOTHER ISLAND, however, for Cuban rum to begin to emerge. The 1790 uprising led by Vincent Ogé on Haiti resulted in a mass exodus of planters from the island. Those who settled in Cuba brought with them knowledge of sugar production and distillation. When the 1791 Haitian Revolution led by François-Dominique Toussaint Louverture started, Cuba was exporting 178,000 gallons of *aguardiente de caña*. By the time it ended, in 1804, Cuban exports reached 1.6 million gallons.

This transformation was aided, in 1796, when the Spanish crown lifted the heavy taxation on Cuban *aguardiente de caña*, which had been imposed to protect the importation of Spanish spirits to the Caribbean after the repeal of the production ban. This reversal of government policy toward rum-making included a crown mandate that required each Cuban sugar refinery owner to install a distillery operation. The largest island in the Caribbean (roughly the same size as England) was finally about to become the largest sugar producer in the world and do so with incredible speed.

By 1864, Cuba exported more
than 4.5 million gallons of rum.

The change was not only seen in the countryside, but in Havana. By the 1820s, what had been a small colonial outpost rose and stretched to become a grand city. The plantocracy built themselves grand houses, ate in fine restaurants and drank in elegant hotels or taverns such as the Piña de Plata (which, in 1867, changed its name to La Florida and later became El Floridita).

The distillate made in their factories was no longer the rotgut given to slaves and bought by all but the upper classes to ward off water-borne illnesses and wash away the pains of hard living. It was a drink to be savored. They even redefined it in the first decade of the nineteenth century. These sophisticates didn't want to drink the *aguardiente de caña* that was downed with an eye-watering grimace by the poor. The tipple they chose was more refined. It was smooth and could be sipped. It was *ron*.

Cuban rum exports, in 1854, accelerated at a remarkable pace. There were a few reasons. That year, Britain opened its ports to foreign produce and commodities, including rum. Western Europe was in the throes of the *oïdium* blight: a vine fungus that devastated vineyards across the continent. With brandy and wine production at a standstill, rum and other spirits were in high demand. Cuba exported nearly three million gallons per year. Six years later, Britain equalized foreign rum import duties, placing Cuban rum producers on par with their British Caribbean competitors. Then the emergence of American sugar syndicates in Cuba during the 1860s stimulated even more rum production.

The Industrial Edge

SUGARCANE EXPLODED from the untouched soils of the Cuban heartland. The timing was advantageous. Cuba's rise coincided with technological advances in science and engineering. Late into the sugar game, Cuban distillers absorbed them all enthusiastically, unlike the older Jamaican, Martinique and Barbados sugar colonies where tradition was hard to shift and new infrastructure investments hard to justify.

The improved steam engine that was developed in the late 1700s by Scottish scientist James Watt changed

the face of industry. Machines replaced the backbreaking work handled by human beings. Watt's invention led to the creation of the steam locomotive, in 1804, by British designers Richard Trevithick and Andrew Vivian. Cargo could now be transported more efficiently by rail than by boat or horse-driven cart.

Cuban sugar producers readily embraced this new technology as they desperately needed it. Sugar production had tripled in the first two decades of the nineteenth century. The first railroad in Latin America was built in Cuba between 1834 and 1837, to transport sugar from the inland to the port of Havana. (In Spain, the first railway—Barcelona-Mataró—was not completed until 1848.) By 1860, there were 400 miles of tracks moving sugarcane.

ABOVE: The steam engine was improved by James Watt, throwing the world into an industrial age.

OPPOSITE: Steam engines such this mid-nineteenth century model offered sugar producers the ability to produced greater amounts of product with reduced manpower.

However, steam had arrived in Cuba prior to the railway's construction. Another enterprising pioneer, Pedro Diago, owner of the Santa Elena plantation and sugar mill is considered to be the father of modern Cuban rum production. Already acclaimed for his innovative farming and processing techniques, in 1818 he imported the second

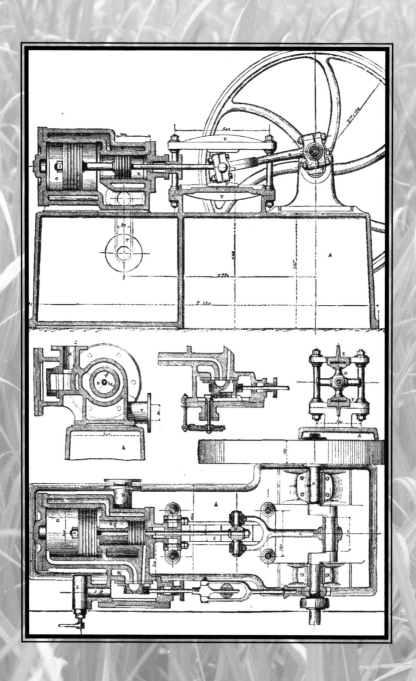

steam engine to Cuba. The first had arrived in 1796 and proved to be a disastrous investment.

However, following Diago's lead, 286 sugar mills installed steam engines in the next eighteen years. That number soared to 961 in the following twenty years, which meant the vast majority of sugarcane was processed using steam-driven machinery. Diago also had the idea of intentionally aging the spirits from his distillery. He did this away from damaging sunlight in pottery jars buried in the earth. He also explored and tested many other innovations to increase and improve production. Though some of his radical concepts were hobbled by technical difficulties of the time that proved insurmountable, the advancements he introduced or popularized revolutionized Cuban rum production. But he was not the only Cuban rum pioneer.

At the turn of the 1800s, all rum was condensed in pot stills: giant copper kettles, which produced a heavy, powerful spirit. This time-honoured distillation method was effective, but time-consuming and inefficient. In 1820, Cuban still-maker Fernando di Arritola radically improved the pot still design usually employed for rum-making. He added a coil to the swan-neck conical head. As Campoamor commented: "de Arritola, using an alembic of his own invention, succeeded in producing a rum superior to its crude Caribbean competitors." Arritola's innovation inspired the entire island. An 1827 survey counted 300 distilleries in Cuba.

A series of inventions developed for use in sugar refinement and whisky-making led to the evolution of the alembic still into the continuous still: first by Jean-Baptiste Cellier-Blumenthal in 1813, then Sir Anthony Perrier in 1822, followed by Robert Stein in 1827 and finally Aeneas Coffey in 1831. These high-volume, fast-output stills were installed by the 1850s into rum distilleries—especially those operating in Cuba.

By 1860, there were approximately 1,365 rum distilleries. Havana publishing houses were printing and distributing books, such as Don Juan Lorenzo Casas's 1860 book *El Manual Teórico Práctico para la Elaboración del Aguardiente de Caña,* to help sugar producers keep apprised the latest improvements in distillation.

The refined spirit we know as Cuban rum was about to be born. Continuous stills were not only more efficient, but produced a new style of rum, one which was light, one which was more in tune with a world whose taste in spirits was changing. New styles appeared: dry, straw-colored

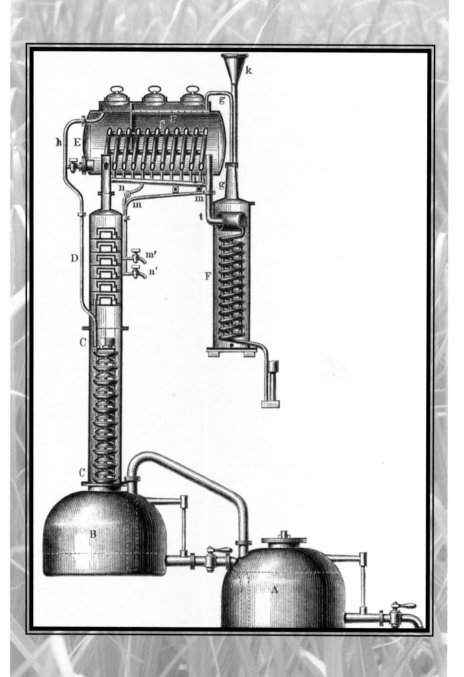

A CRYSTAL-CLEAR SPIRIT

THE WORK OF GERMAN CHEMIST Johann Tobias Lowitz (1757-1804) finally tilted the scales of interest in the use of charcoal in the production of beverage alcohol. In 1785, Lowitz discovered and documented that charcoal adsorbed noxious odors from sick people, putrid meats, and rotting vegetables. He also found the substance was excellent for removing the color from liquids, particularly tartaric acid during its preparation. Honey could be made into a pure sugar by boiling it with powdered charcoal. And by merely shaking corn-based spirit with powdered charcoal, fusel oils and unpleasant esters could be removed, improving the liquor's aroma and taste; any undesirable color would be quickly whisked away, producing a crystal clear product. Not willing to stop there, he tested charcoals made from a variety of woods, documenting which served the best results for the desired purpose.

By 1793, Lowitz accepted a post in St Petersburg, Russia as Professor of Chemistry at the St Petersburg Academy of Sciences. But this did not hinder his obsession with charcoal's transforming effects. Within three years, he successfully collected pure ethyl alcohol by filtering distillate through hardwood charcoal that was activated to increase its adsorption of undesirable particles and aromas.

Lowitz's work caught the eye of a sugar refiner in the British-held Caribbean in 1794, which led to the successful development of crystal clear sugar syrup. But that was the only application of his work he potentially witnessed.

He died before Gruillon opened the first large-scale French sugar refinery to produce clear sugar syrup applying the same process in 1805. That same year, Benjamin Delessert employed charcoal in the production of spirits distilled from sugar beets to improve its appearance and aroma. Napoléon Bonaparte awarded him a Legion of Honour for his efforts.

RIGHT:
Eighteenth-century chemist Johann Tobias Lowitz was the first to discover the clarifying and smoothing properties of charcoal filtration when applied to sugar and spirit production.

LEFT:
Nineteenth-century chemist Benjamin Delessert employed Lowitz's charcoal filtration method to procude a crystal clear, palatable spirit from sugar beets.

C. DEROSNE.

Defecating Cane Juice.

No. 4,108.

Patented July 10, 1845.

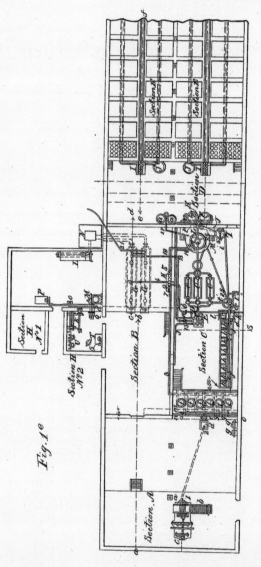

Fig. 1º

FRENCH INDUSTRIALIST CHARLES DEROSNE designed a defecator that used bone-based, activated charcoal to filter impurities out of cane syrup. In 1811, he and partner Charles-Louis Cadet de Gassincourt became the first people to manufacture beet sugar in France, using his device. Twelve years later, Derosne and another partner Jean-François Cali built a filtration machine factory.

Cuba was an early adopter of Derosne's defecator. In addition to this marvelous invention, which heated, decanted, and clarified the can syrup, a sugar mill in the Matanzas region purchased a number of labor-saving machines designed by Derosne and Cali. In 1841, the mill was additionally outfitted with a sugar mill with a mobile mat and vacuum evaporators. Derosne himself came to Cuba to install his equipment as well as train technicians to operate them.

The year before his death in 1846, Derosne finally patented his charcoal filtration invention in the United States and assigned the rights to Patent #4,108 to Joseph F. Lapéra.

Eventually the work of Lowitz and Derosne coupled with the employment of continuous distillation led to the development of a smoother, silvery-hued liquor that became the signature of all Cuban rums.

Carta Blanca; *Carta Oro*, golden in hue; *Ron Palmas*, amber, sweet and aromatic; rich, dark *Añejo*. As these styles developed, so did the world's first real rum brands.

Between 1860 and 1890, numerous brands emerged. Camps Hermanos introduced Ron Matusalem; Fandiño Pérez launched Ron Superior; Crossi Mestre y Cia distilled Ron Crossi y Mestre; Bacardí y Bouteiller SC produced Ron Carta Blanca; JM Parejo introduced Ron Carta Parejo; Trueba Hermanos launched Ron de las Tres Negritas; Rovira y Guillaume distilled Ron Añejo Vencedor.

During the Ten-Year War (1868-1878) that raged along the southeastern rim of Cuba, a new spirit was developed in the northwest, in Cárdenas. Producing spirits at his La Vizcaya distillery in since 1878, Basque-born José Arechabala introduced his Ron Viejo Superior and later produced a special brand called Havana Club.

Cuban rum was revolutionary in execution and in spirit. It's no surprise that its arrival coincided with increased self-awareness on the part of the Cuban people. Cuban distillers may have been the first to truly apply scientific methods to rum making, but they combined this with a passion for their craft. Cuban rum wasn't born in a laboratory. It sprang from the soil of the island, from the souls of a people who forged their own identity, who reveled in their culture, who desired self-determination. If Cuban rum was new, it was because Cuba itself was new.

On 20 May 1902, Cuba gained formal independence from both their Spanish rulers and their temporary American overseers. In a century, the island transformed itself from forgotten colony to a nation, from staging post to the world's biggest sugar producer, from idle distiller to the creator of the style of rum which revolutionized the way in which the world viewed the spirit throughout the twentieth century and into the next.

An International Spirit

JUST BEFORE CUBAN INDEPENDENCE WAS WON, American business interests on the island sprouted and proliferated. Cuba's rich resources of iron ore, tobacco and sugar tantalized power-

THE TEN-YEAR WAR

IT BEGAN ON 10 OCTOBER 1868. A liberal landowner named Carlos Manuel de Céspedes rang the work-bell on his small estate, La Demajagua. When his slaves assembled, he gave a historic speech, the "Grito de Yara" (Cry of Yara). The next day, he read a declaration setting forth Cuba's right to self-government. His *Manifesto de la Junta Revolucionaria de Cuba* became a call to arms.

At first, only a few local planters joined de Céspedes's cause, including Marcos Maceo and his four sons. Three days later, this handful of rebels took eight towns in the surrounding area. Their cause was clearly popular. The small rebel army, which came to be known as the Mambises grew to 12,000 volunteers by the end of the month.

Two years into the fighting, twenty-five year old Antonio Maceo became a lieutenant colonel of the rebel army. Exhibiting remarkable valor and leadership despite the odds, the mestizo Maceo captured the admiration and imagination of Cubans regardless of their ethnic origin. Before the end of the war, he rose to the rank of brigadier general. Fernando Figueredo Socarras recalled Maceo in his 1902 book *La Revolucion de Yara*: "He appeared and disappeared in clouds of smoke and dust, seated on his gigantic horse Concha who responded not to the reins but to the thoughts of his heroic rider; that man, laboring for breath, machete in hand, magnificent embodiment of the angel of destruction, carried out the assault in that battle which for all of us was extraordinary."

The war ended in a stalemate. On 11 February 1878 both sides signed the Treaty of Zanjón. The agreement established that slaves who fought on either side were freed, but that slavery was not abolished. It also stated Cuba was to remain under Spanish rule.

Maceo opposed the treaty because it did not fulfill the goals of the revolution. He expressed his views in a pamphlet titled *The Protest of Baraguá*. Before the year ended, Maceo was appointed by the Acting President of the Republic of Cuba Manuel J Calvar as a Collector of Funds Abroad, putting him in contact with other veterans who were instrumental in the organization of the War of 1895.

ABOVE:
Member of the rebel army
during the Ten-Year War,
Antonio Maceo captured
the admiration and the
imagination of Cubans
regardless of their ethnic
origin.

ful magnates such as JP Morgan and Charles Rand of the Spanish-American Iron Company.

Frequently the early-adopters and drivers of new drink trends, American forces displayed a strong interest in Cuban rum while they were stationed on the island. The United States established a naval base on Guantánamo Bay in 1898 and was granted a perpetual lease on the property five years later. Servicemen on leave flocked to taverns and bars in Santiago de Cuba and Havana to get their fill of Daiquirís, Cuba Libres and other liquid delights.

Not just the privates and corporals took a fancy to rum. Enamored with the Daiquirí after he was introduced to it by Jennings S. Cox Jr. during the Spanish-American War, Admiral Lucius W. Johnson brought the drink home to the Army & Navy Club in Washington DC upon his return to the mainland, in 1909 and imported a generous stock of Cuban rum for his personal consumption.

The 1900s and 1910s also saw the exotic beauty, vibrant sights and hypnotic rhythms of the *camparsa* groups that performed during Carnival in Havana lure thousands of tourists to the island and exposing them to a wide array of rum drinks. That was only the beginning.

The enactment of Prohibition in the United States drew hordes of parched imbibers to Cuba's shores. Havana became America's local bar. A quick flight from Miami or a fishing trip on the Gulf of Mexico brought a thirsty traveler to a haven of Mojitos, Daiquirís, El Presidentes and Cubanitos. Stateside publications fanned the flames of desire. *Travel* Magazine, in 1922, mentioning that "best of all is a Piña Colada, the juice of a perfectly ripe pineapple—a delicious drink in itself—rapidly shaken up with ice, sugar, lime and rum in delicate proportions. What could be more luscious, more mellow and more fragrant?"

Between 1900 and 1919, Cuban rum exports multiplied more than ever before. In 1909 alone, 6,043,252 gallons were produced, of which 1,815,693 gallons were exported.

La Florida, Hotel Nacional, Sloppy Joe's and numerous other establishments hosted wave after wave of intellectuals, motion pictures stars, entertainers, politicians and celebrities. Drinks were crafted by skillful *cantineros* such as Constante Ribalaigua Vert and Maragato in honor of some of their most famous patrons such as Mary Pickford and Greta Garbo.

Repeal of Prohibition did not cease the revelry that could be heard from the Paseo del Prado, along the Malecón and throughout Old Havana. Casinos, nightclubs and the vivacious spirit of the Cuban people continued to attract waves of visitors, hoping to escape a global depression and the threat of another world war. More watering holes opened their doors with welcome arms.

One example was the Havana Club bar, which opened, in 1935, in the former home of the Count of Casa Bayona located on the Plaza de la Cathedral. The *cantineros* there made their concoctions with a brand that bore the same name, Havana Club, which was produced by José Arechabala SA in Cárdenas.

From the 1930s through the 1940s, the party continued, as the world acquired a strong desire for the tropical flavors and aromas of Cuban drinks. Some bar owners commissioned proprietary labels for their rums. Sloppy Joe's and others were brands born from that era.

Songs were even written and recorded about these delights. "Rum and Coca Cola" was one of the most famous of the era, a chart-topping hit for both Xavier Cugat and the An-

If you want to be Right
Invite your Friends with
SLOPPY JOE'S Ron cocktail

WHITE

GOLD
Before you go home don't forget to take a bottle of
SLOPPY JOE'S RON
Ron is guaranteed to be over 12 years old

drews Sisters. Ernest Hemingway and his entourage of Hollywood greats carried the message far and wide. It seemed that the Cuban lifestyle and its rum flowed through the bloodstreams of celebrities and traveled into the mainstream.

The troubled decade of the 1950s heralded unexpected changes both for Cuba and its rum. The revelry had become debauchery under the regime of Fulgencio Bastista. Opening the way for large-scale gambling in Havana, Bastista placed the fate of Cuba and its people in the hands of American big-business interests and American-based organized crime bosses including Meyer Lansky, Santa Trafficante, Thomas Luchcese and Lucky Luciano.

It was during that era, the José Arechabala S.A.—which had become Arechabala Industries—fell into demise. The town of Cárdenas had experienced major setbacks. A plan to deepen town's shallow port never materialized, limiting the company's ability to ship out its products, ranging from candy to sugar to rum. A devastating hurricane, in 1933, struck the area. The cleanup took more than six years to complete.

Between 1940 and 1944, the company's management and manpower were diverted to the task of constructing a modern port and deepening the harbor. By the next decade, the company suffered financial difficulties and wound down its operations. It failed to renew, in 1955, certain of its trademark for its Havana Club rum brand in countries like the United States, Spain or the Dominican Republic.

The allure of Cuban rum took on a mythical status after trade embargoes kept Cuban rum from being exported to one of its largest markets, the United States.

With the overthrow of the Bastista regime by Fidel Castro, in 1959, nationalization of Cuban enterprises ousted foreign control of business on the island. Shareholders and owners who did not agree with nationalization left their businesses, moving to the United States and Europe. Arechabala Industries was one of them.

Empresa Cubana Exportadora de Alimentos y Productos Varios (also known as Cubaexport) took over management of a few time-honored Cuban rums—Matusalem, Ron Santiago, Varadero, Caribbean Club, Los Marinos Patricruzados and Havana Club. It registered the Havana Club trademark in eighty countries, including Spain in 1966 and the United States in 1976. Because Arechabala Industries had not renewed its trademarks in the United States, the Havana Club US trademark became available to any one after its last registration expired in 1973. During the 1970s was built a state-of-the-art distillery in Santa Cruz del Norte, near Havana.

A partnership agreement between the state-owned company Cuba Ron SA and Pernod Ricard, in 1993, changed international perceptions when the brand was revitalized. The success of this venture led to the inauguration, in 2007, of one of the world's largest rum distilleries to specialize in aged rums, located in San José de Las Lajas, near Havana.

Since then, the Havana Club brand has become synonymous with authentic Cuban rum, produced in Cuba with Cuban molasses in the true Cuban rum-making tradition.

CHAPTER THREE

A Living Tradition

THE ART AND ARTISTRY OF MAKING FINE CUBAN RUMS

OPPOSITE:
Havana Club's Primer Maestro
Ronero Don José Navarro admires
a glass of the carefully aged and
blended rum he has crafted.

IT IS A REVERED TRADITION, a tradition that is very much alive in Cuba. It is symphony of rituals executed in four movements, played time and time again by passionate performers before a discerning audience of connoisseurs. This is way fine Cuban rums are made.

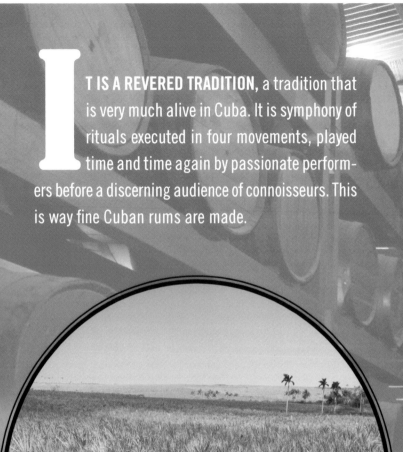

THE SYMPHONIC COMPOSITION that is the classic Cuban rum-making process is played in four movements. The opening "allegro" takes place amid the sights and sounds of harvest time in the lush sugarcane fields that span the length and width of Cuba .

A slow, almost solemn "sonata" sets the pace for the time-honoured ceremonies that transform fresh sugarcane into juice, juice into molasses, molasses into rum. A "rondo" of repetitive tasting and aging steps set out in well-rehearsed score is performed by the *maestro ronero* [master blender] who knows what when subtleties and digressions must executed to achieve the desired crescendo of aromas and flavors.

The fourth and final movement is a lively "scherzo" in which rums are selected and blended into a finale of sensual pleasure that leaves the audience applauding with a resounding "bravo"!

The performers in this orchestra have taken their places on stage. The conductor has taken up his baton. Let the symphony of rum-making begin.

Zafra

THICK, GREEN FIELDS OF RIPE SUGARCANE SPRAWL across the landscape as far as the eye can see: from the Sierra Maestra to the Vuelta Abajo, from Santiago de Cuba to Pinar del Rio.

It is now December. This is when *zafra*—the sugarcane harvest—begins.

The soft rustle of cane leaves swaying in the gentle breeze is punctuated by a whoosh, as blade meets cane stalk. The country hums with the sounds of *macheteros* swinging their machetes into the cane, machinery loading fresh-cut bundles and tractors towing overladen trailers. The railways especially built in the 1800s to transport these precious harvests go into action, speeding the cane towards the towering brick chimneys of the *ingenios* (sugar mills) that punctuate the rural landscape.

Every producing region and each variety of cane grown in Cuba nurtures specific properties. There are people already hard at work, criss-crossing the countryside, selecting the specific types of cane they need to produce a particular type and style of rum while the cane still stands in the fields.

Guarapo to Miel

AFTER THE CANE IS CUT, the *guarapo* [sugarcane juice] is pressed out of the stalk, boiled again and again until it transforms into crystallized sugar. What remains is a thick, rich, sweet substance that Cuban refiners call *miel* [honey].

This is molasses. It is the basic, raw element from which Cuban rum is made. In fact, during the 1700s and 1800s, Cuban molasses was highly-prized by foreign rum producers in North America and Europe, who purchased barrels directly from the sugar mills.

Besides its high 55% sucrose content, Cuban molasses is low in viscosity and acidity as well containing many other favorable qualities that keep it from producing too strong an alcohol that could potentially distort the rum's true character.

The *maestro ronero* carefully selects the molasses to be distilled, which is moved via truck or transport car to the *ronera* [distillery]. At its new home, it is then purified, sterilized and diluted with absolutely pure water. Water, in fact, is the second secret of Cuban rum. Because water makes up the greater portion of the rum recipe, its quality is carefully controlled and guaranteed through a series of precise treatments.

Alchemy

THE MARRIAGE OF MOLASSES AND WATER forms a mixture called *batición*. Another relationship takes places when this liquid meets yeast. It is not the wild yeast used in some distillations such as cachaça or *rhum agricole*. This ingredient has been cultivated and nurtured in the *ronera*'s own laboratory.

Placed in huge vats for about 30 hours, the yeast and *batición* are allowed to naturally ferment under strictly supervised conditions. Microbiologists and physio-chemists assure that the fermentation stays within a safe range that will yield the desired aromas and flavours that are fundamental to the rum's character.

During the distillation process, the fermented liquid endures a long process of repeated evaporation and condensation. The drama plays out in the columns of the continuous still, specially engineered to extract desired qualities that will become Cuban rum. The column still successively purifies the resulting alcohol of undesirable acids, aldehydes and congeners. The *maestro ronero* knows the precise moment

to begin the collection process: when the early alcohols—the "heads"—have been drawn off and the highly-desirable "mids" begin to flow out of the columns. He knows the exact moment the collection must cease to keep the lingering "tails" from influencing the bouquet of the *aguardiente*: its aromas and flavours.

The Fortress

THE FRAGRANCE OF RICH OAK WOOD spices the humid air. Entire ramparts of 180-litre casks—shored up by bracing—rise to impressive heights. In the heart of these fortresses of rum, it is not unusual to be struck with awe by the vision, by the atmosphere, by the promise of things that will transpire within the casks themselves. This is where the true magic of Cuban rum takes place.

The *ronera*'s position is ideally situated: the humidity levels and temperature favor perfect aging conditions. Everything in the *ronera*'s aging cellars is monitored: the quality of the American white oak casks previously used to age bourbon, their age, climate fluctuations that occur during the aging process, the ventilation of the cellar itself via latticed windows. There will be an "angel's share" that will escape during aging. The heat and humidity of the tropical Cuban climate means a larger portion of angel's share than found in whisky

OPPOSITE: Old American white oak casks are carefully chosen for use in the rum aging process. Some barrels used for the end of the process are nearly a century old.

or cognac will be sacrificed. Nevertheless, it is a small price to pay for the final, ecstatic results.

Añejamiento

IN THE FIRST PHASE OF AGING, the *aguardiente* rests for a minimum of 18 months, enough time to create a "soul": a relationship between aromas and flavours of both the spirit and the wood.

Unique to Cuban rum since the mid-1800s, the rested *aguardiente* is allowed to pass drop-by-drop through casks that contain various layers of activated charcoal. The process removes unwanted aromas and flavors, readying it for its next phase of identification and further aging. The *aguardiente* is then mixed with pure sugarcane distillate to produce what is called *ron fresco* [young rum] and put to age once more time.

This is when the art of the *maestro ronero* reaches its peak. Deep in the *ronera*'s cellars, he opens each cask, tastes and determines its future. Some are destined to be blended elaborate the less-aged *añejo blanco*: light, warm rum, transparent and as flavorful as fresh sugarcane juice. Others are chosen to be come *madres* [mothers] who will undergo further *añejamiento*, the secondary aging, bound to become an *añejo*, the epitome of the Cuban rum spectrum.

in his flock. His disciple accompanies him, committing to memory the story behind each and every cask.

Constantly refining an organoleptic perception in a mute sensorial dialogue over the years, *maestro* and his disciple arrive at a perfect symbiosis in their choices of casks as well as the method in which they will be blended. A balance in aromas and flavours, coupled with consistency, is the ultimate goal.

Backed by a panel of a dozen experienced tasters who regularly analyze the qualities of each batch of rum, the *maestro* tastes and does not spit in the fashion well-known amongst vintners. Fine Cuban rum must be swallowed to appreciate its finish. After this tasting, each rum is then chemically and biologically analyzed by a team of experts who precisely determine potential development of each batch. Each cask has its own distinctive character and possesses a privileged destiny.

OPPOSITE:
Two barrels of aged rum are blended together and then sampled.

**Nothing is added to the rums
to make this miracle happened.**

There are no caramels, artificial flavorings or colorants added to these *añejos* that were born in the cane fields, concentrated in the sugar mills into molasses, distilled and aged in the *ronera* to achieve their natural beauty.

After each fixed interval in the *añejamiento* process, the *maestro ronero* executes a subtle blending session. The final touch. The *toque*. It is a delicate moment, in which the *maestro ronero* puts all his experience and know-how to the test. Under his orders, the cellar workers roll the barrels before him, open the taps and allow marvelous streams of two amber, aromatic liquids run together.

After settling for several weeks, each of these custom blends finds its balance and harmony. The *maestro ronero*'s rums now possess definitive personalities. Does this cask become an aged cocktail rum? Is it a sipping rum? Or is it a spiritual experience to be enjoyed by true connoisseurs? Does it need more time to achieve its true character? Only the *maestro ronero* knows the heart and soul of each cask as well as the blends he orchestrated in this symphony of aromas and flavors that is authentic Cuban rum.

But the artistic process does not end there. Cuban bottlers have an understandable reverence for these prestigious rums that are *hecho en Cuba* [made in Cuba]. These smiling young women, with their lively speech and communicative courtesy, work quickly and efficiently to smooth a label, or check the appearance of each bottle. Accompanied by a parting burst of good humor: another Cuban rum is ready to enter the world.

There is only one way to know that a bottle of Cuban rum is authentic. Look for the seal of authenticity issued by the Cuban government which must be affixed to each and every bottle that is exported. Besides demonstrating the pride with which these rums are made, this label assures consumers that the contents is a premium quality, genuine Cuban rum that is produced in Cuba, distilled from Cuban molasses, filtered and aged according to traditional Cuban methods. Accept nothing less.

CHAPTER FOUR

Eyes, Nose & Mouth

EXPERIENCING THE AROMAS AND FLAVORS OF FINE CUBAN RUMS

OPPOSITE:
Primer Maestro Ronero Don José Navarro admires a bottle of Havana Club Añejo 7 Años during a tasting session.

TASTING RUM—just like experiencing fine wine, whisky, or cognac—commands the use of a distinctive vocabulary. Like the music in Havana's streets, Cuban rum plays on the palate in major chords rather than single notes. It tantalizes the eyes with its range of colors. It delights the nose with its bouquets. It coaxes the palate, inspiring a profusion of descriptive verses from the first sip to the long finish. Once the final notes have been played, rum can be savored and enjoyed responsibly in memory for years to come.

THERE ARE AS MANY DIFFERENCES amongst *añejos* as there are among whiskeys and whiskies. The quality of the *rons frescos*, the condition of the casks, the temperature of the cellar and the time spent aging in the cellar are all variables to be considered in an *añejo*'s evaluation. Perceiving these differences is more a matter of training than talent. Here are a few tips from the experts in conducting a proper tasting.

The Environment

A PROPER *AÑEJO* TASTING should be conducted in an odor-free, well-lit room that has at least one bright-white surface (a table, a wall, or even a napkin) that can serve as a backdrop for viewing each sample. Participants should also be odor-free (no heavy perfumes, colognes and deodorants) and should not consume any strong flavors (coffee, garlic, pungent spices) for at least thirty minutes before a tasting.

Evaluate each *añejo* sample at room temperature (75° to 78° degrees Fahrenheit / 23° to 25° Celsius) and at full strength. Use a standard white wine glass or a specially-made tasting glass that is clean and free of soap residue, bleached drying cloth and other aromas.

Pour approximately 1 ounce (30 ml) of *añejo* into the tasting glass. Then, one-by-one, follow the sensory evaluation steps in the following order: sight, smell, taste and touch.

Tasting with the Eyes

HOLD THE GLASS IN FRONT of a bright-white backdrop. Check that your sample is dust-free and particulate-free. Assess the color. Does it have a silvery cast or a pale golden hue? Is it deep golden or dark as caramel?

Lightly swirl the *añejo* around the glass. This opens up the aromas by increasing the surface-area-to-volume ratio of *añejo* in the glass. By doing this, the glycerol content can also be judged. As the *añejo* sinks back into the glass, look for a thick appearance that indicates how the *añejo* will rest on the tongue: will it be viscous or thin? Glimpse the degree of richness and fullness that you will feel on the palate. Some authorities say that if the *añejo* streams down the sides of the glass in a rosary-bead chain of small drops, it has a higher alcohol level. The bigger the beads, the lighter the spirit content.

OPPOSITE: Navarro knows that the first taste is with the eyes.

Tasting with the Nose

BRING THE RIM OF THE GLASS UP just under your nose and open your mouth below the rim. Then inhale through your nose only. This allows the aroma to swirl across the back and top of your palate, where it reaches additional receptors. To experience the difference, try smelling the *añejo* with your mouth closed. You'll soon discover that open- and closed-mouth

tasting are radically different. There are subtle aromas that can only be detected with your mouth open.

Tasting with the Tongue

JUST LIKE FINE WINE, fine *añejo* should be "chewed". Slosh the *añejo* around in your mouth and inhale across it to bring out the full flavors. After the initial "chew", bring the glass back up to your nose to round out the flavor experience. Some purists may balk at this. However, the idea is not to separate taste and smell, but to gain the fullest possible sensory experience. Next, judge the taste three ways: on its composition; on its intensity; and on its duration or finish.

Tasting with the Mouth

MOST PEOPLE TEND TO FORGET that this fourth sense is also involved in sensory evaluation. The rum's mouth feel can reveal points of quality, which aren't as apparent in its aroma or taste. Warmth versus a burning alcohol feel is a perfect example. A viscose texture is another. Is the rum thin and astringent leaving the mouth feeling drier than before you tasted it? Or does it coat the palate?

Now, come and acquaint yourself with these new skills by experiencing Havana Club *añejos*. Your host Don José Navarro will provide comments and tasting notes.

Havana Club Añejo Blanco

"To my knowledge, Havana Club Añejo Blanco is the whitest of all aged rums and the most aged of all white rums."—Don José Navarro

EYES: Clear with light sun-colored tones born from aging in white oak barrels.

NOSE: A fresh, easy aroma, reminiscent of vanilla and cherry, with a hint of fresh cocoa.

TONGUE/MOUTH: A balanced, subtle character, possessing both sweet and fruity notes as well as a crisp finish.

SERVICE: The perfect spirit for mixing refreshing drinks such as the traditional Cuban national cocktail, the Mojito.

*Havana Club
Añejo 3 Años*

"Havana Club Añejo 3 Años, light and dry, with persistent taste and aroma, is ideal for a luxury Daiquirí."
—Don José Navarro

EYES: A pleasant 'light straw' color. Bright, clear and dense, revealing the qualities of its age.

NOSE: An assertive nose with accents of vanilla, caramelized pears, banana and hints of smoked oak.

TONGUE/MOUTH: A very smooth, pleasant palate, with smoky, vanilla and chocolate notes.

SERVICE: The perfect ingredient in classic cocktails such as the Floridita Daiquirí, adding prestige and refinement. Slightly drier than Añejo Blanco, it can also be enjoyed neat or over ice.

Havana Club
Añejo Especial

"Havana Club Añejo Especial whispers the hidden secrets of premium dark aged rums."—Don José Navarro

EYES: A warm, mesmerizing golden hue.

NOSE: An intense aroma, reminiscent of sugarcane with slightly smoky accents and hints of honey, vanilla and cinnamon.

TONGUE/MOUTH: An intense rum with well-rounded balance.

FINISH: A lingering and smooth finish.

SERVICE: A versatile golden rum that is the perfect feature in classic Cuban cocktails such as the Cuba Libre. It can also be enjoyed straight or on the rocks.

Havana Club Añejo Reserva

"Havana Club Añejo Reserva is a miracle of complexity and extreme smoothness. That makes it a dark aged rum that is easy to drink and share. Añejo Reserva is the perfect rum to offer and share."—Don José Navarro

EYES: A warm and radiant amber hue.

NOSE: Integrated aromas of caramel, pear and light tobacco introduce a more robust bouquet of aromatic wood notes: the result of natural aging.

TONGUE/MOUTH: A spirit with strong character that open to complex, lasting aromas of cacao, coffee, tobacco and spices.

FINISH: Impressively round and smooth.

SERVICE: Exceptional in a Cuba Libre or other classic Cuban cocktails that call for aged rum. It can also be enjoyed neat or on the rocks.

Havana Club
Añejo 7 Años

"Havana Club Añejo 7 Años is the rum which I am most
proud of. It is the very essence of aged Cuban rum.
Having the responsibility to always maintain it at its
top quality level, I feel a strong personal and emotional
connection with it."—Don José Navarro

EYES: A dazzling, deep mahogany hue.

NOSE: An exquisite bouquet with intense and complex notes
of cocoa, vanilla, cedar, sweet tobacco and lush tropical fruits.

TONGUE/MOUTH: A stylish and exceptionally rich rum with
a voluptuous, silky entry that leads to a balanced yet extraordinarily complex palate with notes of rich brown
spice.

FINISH: Intense yet round and smooth. Its complex notes
combine with a crispness reminiscent of its sugarcane
origins.

SERVICE: Can be enjoyed neat, however the complexity of the
aroma can be drawn out by adding an ice cube, or by allowing it to breathe for a few minutes in the glass. Alternatively, it can be used in a truly indulgent Cuba Libre.
Matches beautifully with a fine Havana cigar.

Havana Club Barrel Proof

"Havana Club Cuban Barrel Proof is a unique rum that transports you to our legendary '*naves de añejamiento*' –the Havana Club aging cellars."—Don José Navarro

With Havana Club Barrel Proof, Don Navarro conceived a unique concept in rum: bottled straight from the barrel at 45% ABV. He skillfully combined the lightness and smoothness of a delicate, classic sipping rum with the intensity and complexity of carefully aged rum.

EYES: A warm amber hue, with a deep red glow.

NOSE: Light caramel, toasted pecan and spice aromas which open to more robust origins with tobacco and wood notes.

TONGUE/MOUTH: A round and buoyant entry leads to a complex, flavourful, full-bodied palate of dark caramel, cocoa, coffee, sweet tobacco and brown spices.

FINISH: A pleasant smoky oak and spice finish blends with caramelized fruits.

SERVICE: A slow sipping rum meant to be enjoyed neat or on the rocks. Matches beautifully with a fine Havana cigar.

Havana Club
Añejo 15 Años

"Cuban rum's great classic"—Don José Navarro

EYES: A bright, intense amber hue that makes it a vibrant, "glowing rum".

NOSE: A long, lingering aroma that is smooth, refreshing, filled with ripe fruit.

TONGUE/MOUTH: The first impression ranges from honey to dried plum. The second expresses banana, pear, fresh and dried fig, on an incredibly smooth and delicate oak base with light acidity.

FINISH: A long-lasting finish refreshes the throat with hints of chocolate-coated mature coconut.

SERVICE: As befits a great classic *añejo*, it is best showcased neat, preferably in a snifter. Matches beautifully with a fine Havana cigar.

Havana Club Máximo Extra Añejo

"Havana Club Máximo Extra Añejo is the supreme expression of Cuban rum."—Don José Navarro

Blending the oldest reserve rums and *aguardientes* found in the Havana Club aging cellars, generations of Cuban *maestro roneros* and their work are showcased to best express the finest of traditional Cuban rum making.

EYES: An impressively deep, dark amber glow.

NOSE: An outstandingly rich, intense, persistent yet delicate aroma with unparalleled complexity, balancing notes of oak and smokiness with subtle tones of fresh pear, coconut and dried fruit.

TONGUE/MOUTH: Robust yet velvety smooth. Both dry and sweet, its woody palate imparts a silky opulence with a cascade of flavors accented by dark chocolate, dried fruits and a hint of vanilla.

FINISH: A warm enduring finish, with irresistible spicy notes and uncommon persistence.

SERVICE: A slow sipping *añejo* that is intended to be savored neat, preferably after dinner. A memorable experience when matched with a fine Havana cigar.

CHAPTER FIVE

Los Cantineros

CLASSIC CUBAN BAR AND BARTENDERS

OPPOSITE:
A cantinero at Bar
Havana Club, located
in the Museo del
Ron in Old Havana,
vigorously shakes
a Cuban classic
cocktail.

RUM FITS CUBA like a fine leather glove. The nation touched by so many cultures has assimilated each and every one of them to weave an intricate tapestry all its own. Cubans possess a humor, a compassion and a *joie de vivre* that quickly and effectively smooth any friction that could arise when people from so many different horizons settle in one place. Rum is one of the unifiers of Cuban culture. No matter what their origin or their station in life, all Cubans are proud of their rum: it is a national treasure.

HAVANA AT THE TURN of the twentieth century was known as the "Little Paris of the Caribbean," and according to MC Touchard, the author of *L'Aventure du Rhum,* it was a privileged enclave where rum brought together the world's most famous actors, best-selling authors, idle heirs and a variety of personalities that weren't yet called the jet set. The bars, the *cantineros* [bartenders] who presided over them and even the drinks themselves all have fascinating tales to tell.

Sloppy Joe's

NO LESS THAN 37 STOOLS and all are taken! Such was the impressive spectacle that lay before Sloppy Joe's two master *cantineros*. This perennially crowded bar on Animas Street between Prado and Zulueta Streets was a requisite destination from the 1930s to the 1950s for any visitor to Havana.

José Abeal y Otero arrived in Havana from Spain in 1904 and took a bartending job at the corner of Galiano and Zanja Streets. After three years, he packed his bags and set sail for New Orleans where he honed his skills behind the bar. Then he stopped in Miami where he continued to practice his craft.

As the legend was told in the 1936 *Sloppy Joe's Cocktail Manual*:

> *In the year 1918, he returned to Havana and got a
> job as a bartender at a café named 'Greasy Spoon'*

and six months after, he decided to go into business for himself and bought what was then an insignificant bodega *[grocery store] at the same corner now occupied by Sloppy Joe's.*

While operating this small grocery store, he was visited by several of his old friends from the States. It so happened that while some of them were visiting him and seeing the poor appearance and filthy looking condition of the place one of them said: "Why Joe, this place is certainly sloppy. Look at the filthy water running from under the counter."

Nestled between the fashionable Plaza and Sevilla hotels, José and his partner Valentin Garcia initially sold liquor and sundry groceries. Business developed rapidly and in a very short time, they opened the elongated bar.

Sloppy Joe's had a reputation. One day, an American journalist who lost a wad of money during one drinking session was quite moved and grateful to find his wallet and its entire contents at the bar the next day.

Thanks to this news item, American servicemen based in San Antonio de los Banos made Sloppy Joe's one of their regular hangouts. As soon as they arrived in the trusted establishment, the GIs put their money on the bar and start drinking. As drinks were served, the *cantineros* drew payment from the stack until the funds ran out or the drinkers staggered out.

"Daiquirís and Piña Con Ron were the favorite orders," recalled Fabio, one Sloppy Joe's *cantinero*. "We made them in gigantic shakers and sometimes we made as many as a hundred at a time. The customers loved that and would order a round for the whole house!" This was an idiosyncrasy of the exuberant American millionairess Amelia Rusakoe, who made Sloppy Joe's her headquarters.

For four decades, rich, famous and anonymous clients gathered for Sloppy Joe's giant cocktails—made with its own proprietary-label rum—and listened to the strains of "Vereda Tropical" and other languorous *boleros* played by the house *trovadores*.

La Bodeguita del Medio

◇◇◇◇◇◇◇◇◇◇◇◇◇◇◇◇◇◇

IT IS NOT THE OLDEST ALTAR to classic Havana cocktails, but La Bodeguita del Medio is one of the most famous in the annals of Cuban rum history. Its story began in 1942 when the son of modest farmers, Angel Martinez, purchased an old, rustic *bodega* called La Complaciente situated on Calle Empedrado in Old Havana. Patiently, he renovated the shop himself and renamed it Casa Martinez. He catered to his neighbors' needs, selling rum, soda, rice and beans. That is, until 1946, when he met his new neighbor, publisher Felito Ayon. Because he produced the influential *Arte y Literatura* magazine, Havana's *avant garde* were his business and social milieu. He later recalled his first encounter with Angel:

OPPOSITE:
La Bodeguita del Medio is a cocktail institution in Old Havana.

> *I met Angel Martinez as soon as I set up in Calle Empedrado. Since I didn't have a phone yet, I called my clients from Casa Martinez. At that time it was a simple grocery store, but Angel also served refreshments. Little by little, I began taking my visitors there for a drink.*

Two years later, the two men solidified a close friendship. Ayon was invited to traditional *criollo* lunch cooked by Martinez's wife Armenia. A plate of fried pork chunks with garlic, rice and black beans cost a mere peso. Angel would accept no more than that.

How did the establishment get its name? Ayon phoned a friend one day to ask her to lunch: "Meet me in a *bodeguita* [little *bodega*] in the *medio* [middle] of the block." Soon he and all his friends referred to Martinez's place by this phrase of endearment. The unassuming owner gave in to their insistence and renamed his establishment La Bodeguita del Medio.

Many of Havana's best drinking establishments and luxury hotels offered Mojitos in those days: La Concha, Floridita, El Central. Yet Martinez's particular recipe for Mojitos captured the hearts and palates of novelist Ernest Hemingway, performer Nat King Cole, actor Errol Flynn, writer Gabriel Garcia Marquez and actress Brigitte Bardot, maintaining its international adoration to this day.

El Floridita

NO VISIT TO HAVANA would be complete without a cocktail, or two, or three at El Floridita: *La Cuna Del Daiquirí* [The Cradle of the Daiquirí]. Its motto is proudly emblazoned in bronze letters displayed behind the bar and its statement remains unchallenged. Although the Daiquirí Natural has its roots in the thirst-quenching Cancháncharra, it was at El Floridita that the Daiquirí Frappé evolved and gained worldwide attention.

El Floridita's neo-classical *criollo* décor, with columns framing a mural that depicts Old Havana, a long bar, staffed with impeccably uniformed bartenders and an elegant dining room made it a regular pitstop for the sophisticated and the fashionable. Its glamorous image was such that *Esquire Magazine* compared it to the Ritz in Paris, the Long Bar at Raffles in Singapore and Club 21 in New York.

Originally opened as the *bodega* La Piña de Plata [The Silver Pineapple], in 1820, the spot quickly became a meeting place for VIPs and politicians who frequented the nearby El Capitolio, Cuba's national capital building. Even before Don Narciso Sala Parera took it over in 1898, the establishment's named was changed to La Florida. Regulars expressed their fondness for it by using the diminutive "La Floridita".

Although most Havana *cantineros* made their cocktails icy cold by shaking them in a two-part or three-part shaker set, Parera trained his staff to mix their drinks the old fashioned way, rolling the liquid from one mixing glass to another while stabilizing the ice with a julep strainer held over one of the glasses. (His cousin Miguel Boadas carried this tradition with him when he emigrated to Barcelona in 1925 and within a few years opened Spain's first cocktail bar Las Boadas, off the bustling Las Ramblas. Boadas's daughter

Maria Dolores and her staff still employ the same technique today at the now famous establishment.)

OPPOSITE:
A statue of Ernest Hemingway now sits at El Floridita in the same spot the author occupied for nearly two decades.

Around 1918, Constantino Ribalaigua Vert became its proprietor, the creator of celebrated cocktails such as El Presidente, Mary Pickford and Mulata. Already a celebrity watering hole, Constante changed its name to El Floridita just before its reputation was elevated to landmark status when, in 1938, Ernest Hemingway took up residence on the block.

The tale goes that Hemingway took a break from writing one day and stopped into El Floridita at the other end of the street, where he ordered a Daiquirí from Constante and became an instant regular. The rest is the stuff of legend.

Constante

◇◇◇◇◇◇◇◇◇◇◇◇◇◇◇◇

CONSTANTINO RIBALAIGUA VERT was born in the Catalonian coastal village of Lloret del Mar, on northeastern Spain's Costa Brava. The son of a poor fisherman, Ribalaigua emigrated to Havana in 1914 and went to work immediately as a *cantinero*. Accessible, amiable, admirable, his clients called him "Constante" [Constant], as he worked the room from table to table. According to Fernando Campoamor, Ribalaigua appeared at his post, "like a juggler coming into the ring, with black trousers, white shirt, string tie, tuxedo jacket and an apron".

He performed his magic before a star-studded audience: the Duke of Windsor, the boxer Gene Tunney, actor Gary Cooper, philosopher Jean-Paul Sartre, matador Louis Miguel Dominguin, novelist Tennessee Williams, actor Spencer Tracy, heavyweight champion Rocky Marciano, actress Marlene Dietrich and hundreds more.

Constante brandished the limes taken from his special cache. He squeezed them high above the bar, like a magician pulling a rabbit from this hat. Ava Gardner would swoon at the sight.

A Hundred Cocktails

◇◇◇◇◇◇◇◇◇◇◇◇◇◇◇◇◇◇◇◇◇◇◇◇◇◇◇◇◇◇◇◇◇◇◇◇◇◇

LIKE A GREAT FRENCH CHEF, Constante became a role model for his profession. Fueled by his inspiration and pride in their craft, the *cantineros* created a professional organization: the *Asociacion de Cantineros de Cuba*. Founded in 1924, the association was subsidized by local distilleries, brasseries and liquor merchants. Their initial headquarters was situated below Paseo del Prado, in the heart of Havana's grand hotel district and it quickly grew. The *cantineros* talent was so highly appreciated, that their sponsors competed to improve the association's facilities, adding a billiard table, a library and even a jai alai court. At one point, the association even owned a bathing establishment in Boca Ciega, east of Havana.

OPPOSITE: This manual, produced by the Asociacion de Cantineros de Cuba, in 1948, taught young bartenders the art of service as well as cocktail making.

The *Asociacion de Cantineros de Cuba* also served a trade unionizing role. It defended the interests of its members and provided apprenticeships. The junior *cantineros* took English courses: indispensable for serving a prominent American and British clientele. To qualify, a journeyman

A MILITANT CANTINERO

LIKE THE *CANTINEROS* who grew up and worked the chic and sophisticated Havana of yesteryear, Elio Moya has many strong and mixed memories of the times when the Cuban capital rang with the clinking of glasses and chips as they fell on the gaming tables at the city's casinos.

His memories reflect back to the time he spent behind the bar of La Torre Restaurant, on the top floor of the Focsa Building, whose bay windows still offer a unique panorama of Havana. One of his regular customers was US Ambassador Philip Bonsail. President of the *Asociacion de Cantineros de Cuba* in that murky time of political effervescence, Elio was a militant during the growing revolution. And in this context, he exerted the legendary professional discretion of the *cantineros*, keeping an attentive ear perked during happy hour as he served up Daiquiris and Ron Collinses to a full roster of international diplomats.

The scene changes to a different bar, a different atmosphere.

The Eden Roc, a Vedado nightclub, was exclusively reserved for casino bosses, croupiers and other casino personnel. Although the owner of the Eden Roc—a former bartender at the Eden Roc in Miami—was informed of the revolutionary activities of his recently-hired *cantinero*, Elio found himself behind the bar, experiencing the civility, sophistication, and generous tips of the most powerful American organized-crime bosses: Santos Trafficante, Meyer Lansky, and Lefty Clark.

OPPOSITE:
President of the *Asociacion de Cantineros de Cuba* during the 1950s, Elio Moya served both dignitaries and crime bosses during his long career as a *cantinero*.

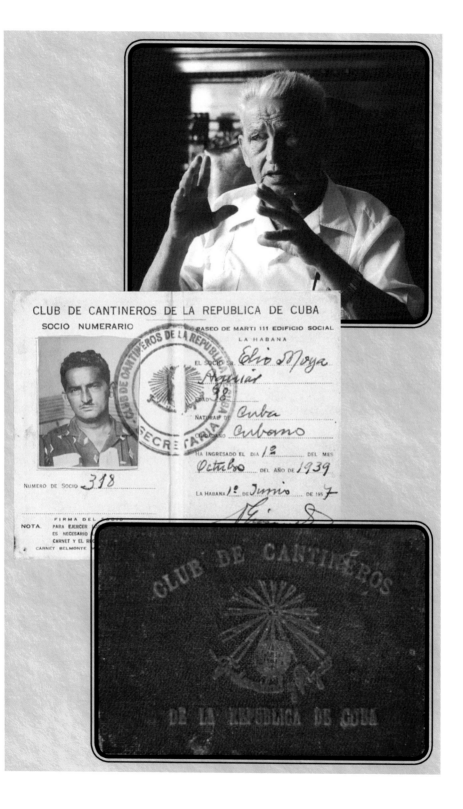

CLUB DE CANTINEROS DE LA REPUBLICA DE CUBA

SOCIO NUMERARIO

PASEO DE MARTI 111 EDIFICIO SOCIAL

LA HABANA

EL SOCIO SR. _Elio Moya_

Aguiar

EDAD _98_

NATURAL DE _Cuba_

CIUDADANO _Cubano_

HA INGRESADO EL DIA _1º_ DEL MES

Octubro DEL AÑO DE _1939_

LA HABANA _1º_ DE _Junio_ DE 195_7_

NUMERO DE SOCIO _318_

FIRMA DEL SOCIO

NOTA. PARA EJERCER

ES NECESARIO

CARNET Y EL RE

CARNET BELMONTE

CLUB DE CANTINEROS

DE LA REPUBLICA DE CUBA

cantinero had to know the recipes for a hundred cocktails from memory.

The association conducted an annual competition that took place in one of the Havana hotels: a formal ritual with strict rules, but with a twist. The jury was chosen not only from among industry professionals, but select civilians, "new palates" who were as passionate about cocktails as the contestants. They added freshness and an essential connection with the customers, to the proceedings.

The *Asociacion de Cantineros de Cuba* still exists today: a living reminder of the great contributions Cuban bartenders have made to the levels of creativity and professionalism in the industry. The association continues to fulfill its role in defending and demonstrating the profession of *cantinero* and contributes more than ever to the international promotion of authentic Cuban Rum and its leading brand, Havana Club.

With the support of the brand, the association's cocktail competitions continue throughout the country. Every two years, a grand national final is held in Havana alternating with the most awaited Havana Club International Cocktail Grand Prix, which also honors the style, inventiveness and expertise of these cocktail masters, who come from all over the world. It provides an excellent forum for showcasing Cuban cocktail making to professionals who have led the cocktail revival in major metropolises around the globe. And offers cantineros an opportunity to be inspired by new influences that will blossom into future Cuban classics.

Bartender's Sixth Sense

Journalist Hector Zumbado best described the *cantinero*'s skills and expertise when he wrote:

> *Diplomatic, polyglot, like skilled ambassadors. Discreet and reserved...They have a good feel for psychology and a deep understanding of human nature. They are father-confessors, competent advisors on a multitude of complex and delicate issues. They are stoics, capable of enduring with unlimited comprehension and courtesy, all the incoherence of the mad world that sometimes condenses in a bar.*

> *They have the elegance of a symphony conductor, the precision and calm of a surgeon ready to operate. They are the chemists of today, the botanists of the eighteenth century, the alchemists of the Middle Ages, capable of willing the creation of cool, shining gold. They are experts in the topics of sport and international politics, but they never give in to passionate discourse. They are philosophers and when need be, telepaths...and to top it off, they need the memory of elephants..."*

CHAPTER SIX

Cocktail Legends

CLASSIC CUBAN COCKTAILS

OPPOSITE:
The *cantinero*'s essential
tools—a shaker, a measure,
and a strainer—are used
to make a myriad of classic
Cuban cocktails.

FEW PEOPLE REALIZE how many classic cocktails were invented in Cuba, beyond the Mojito, Daiquirí and Cuba Libre. A quick flight from Miami to Cuba or a fishing trip on the Gulf of Mexico or the Caribbean brought a thirsty traveler to a haven of El Presidentes, Mulatas, Cubanitos, Mary Pickfords and a precursor to the Piña Colada—Saocos. It was a particularly welcome sight for parched patrons during Prohibition in the United States. Before the 1959 Revolution, Havana was many Americans' "local bar." Stateside publications fanned the flames of desire. *Travel* Magazine, in 1922, mentioned a rum-based cocktail consumed in Cuba since the 19th Century, that took off thirty years later, albeit in a different form: the Piña Colada, a simple blend of rum, fresh pineapple juice and lime juice.

THROUGHOUT THE CENTURIES, masterful *cantineros* have served up a repertoire as legendary in its history as the icons of entertainment, literature, music, politics and business who drank them. *Piropos*—flattering compliments for which the Latin temperament is famed—were whispered from one debonair customer to a lovely other. With a raised glass, a *piropo* is toasted to the *cantinero* for his creation. A *trovador* receives a *piropo* from a sultry listener whose heart echoes in murmurs the soft strum of his guitar.

As sunset gives way to night, the hour of the *borrachera*, the intoxication of the soul, begins. Beginning with the legends surrounding three of the world's favorite Cuban cocktails, more than a dozen scintillating sips are presented here to enhance the magic of any evening.

Mojito

THE MOJITO IS A TRULY CUBAN DRINK, mingling African and European cultures into a spellbinding, invigorating concoction. In West Africa, a *mojo* is a cloth bag filled with magic spices and articles crafted to cast a spell. The word "mojito" is the diminutive of this loan-word and means "little spell." Mojitos have cast a spell on the world for centuries in one liquid form or another. It is the direct descendant of a libation favoured by pirates and privateers, especially one in particular.

OPPOSITE:
The refreshing
Mojito evolved from
a pirate's favorite
beverage into a true
Cuban classic.

Legend has it that one of the earliest concoctions in cocktail history was invented in honor of a sixteenth-century British privateer, known best for his exploits along the Spanish Main. A hero in the eyes of Britain's Queen Elizabeth I, Sir Francis Drake was the scourge of the Spanish Crown, who dubbed him "El Draque" [the Dragon]. During the 1570s and 1580s, Drake and his crew, which included French sailors and *cimarrones* (sometimes also known as Maroons, African slaves who escaped from sugar plantations) took up privateering as a profession. This was a "legitimized" form of piracy sanctioned by the Queen herself. From the Caribbean and the South American coast up to western Canada, Drake plundered Spanish galleons laden with Peruvian gold and claimed portions of the North American coastline in the name of Britain.

Some stories claim that pirate Richard Drake invented a drink, which he named after his boss El Draque. The basic concoction included readily available ingredients from a pirate's point of view: sugar, limes, *aguardiente de caña* and a variety of mint known locally as *hierba buena*: a red-stemmed mint with the scientific name *mentha suaveolens,* which is commonly known as apple mint, woolly mint, or Cuban mint.

Campoamor detailed that El Draque was given this potion as a medicinal to settle his stomach, affected by the tropical climate and diet. Even after El Draque's death in

1596, Drakes or Draquecitos were taken as a refreshing break to the day.

When did the Draquecito evolve into the Mojito? According to author Ciro Bianchi Ross and historian Miguel Bonera, the Mojito Batido first appeared in print around 1910 and was served at La Concha in Havana. By that time, commercial ice had been imported and then produced in the city for nearly a hundred years. Havana's cantineros relished serving icy cold drinks. Muddling the fragrant mint, adding crystal clear ice and topping it with soda water transformed the El Draque into a refreshment deserving a name of special merit.

Many of Havana's finest hotels and bars embraced the Mojito in the first decades of the twentieth century. But it was the hands of Angel Martinez at La Bodeguita del Medio and celebrity promotion by novelist Ernest Hemingway shaped the drink into an international legend.

MOJITO CRIOLLO

IT IS IMPORTANT to remember that the Mojito is an aromatized Rum Collins or Rickey. Many bartenders try to rusticate the recipe by muddling lime in the drink rather than using fresh lime juice or try to substitute brown sugar for white. These create interesting drinks but not Mojitos. The best Cuban versions always use lime juice and white castor sugar. The use of castor sugar is important as it acts as an abrasive on the mint releasing it's fragrant oils without it being necessary to totally pulverize it as it so often the case. Also cracked rock ice is most appropriate not crushed ice, the dilution comes from the addition of soda. Crushed ice merely pulverizes the mint creating a green soup.

INGREDIENTS
50ml Havana Club Añejo 3 Años or Añejo Blanco
25ml Fresh squeezed lime juice
3 teaspoons Castor sugar
6-8 mint leaves and two complete stems of mint

METHOD
First add the mint leaves and the sugar to a highball glass. Then add the fresh lime juice and stir to dissolve and release the mint aromas. Then add the rum. At this point if possible leave the drink to infuse for a few minutes, perhaps while you make other drinks. Finally fill the glass with cracked rock ice and a splash of soda. Gently use a barspoon to mix the ingredients. Garnish with 2 stems of freshly cut mint, thus allowing the mints juice to run into the drink. Slap the mint to release it's fragrance and serve with straws cut to the height of the garnish.

Daiquirí

◇◇◇◇◇◇◇◇◇◇◇◇◇◇◇

THE DAIQUIRÍ HAS VERY CLOSE ASSOCIATIONS with Cuba's fight for independence, from its birth through its evolution into the world's most beloved Cuban cocktail. The first cry for independence, in 1868, was sounded at Yara, near Santiago de Cuba and echoed through the nearby mining village of Daiquirí.

In their bid for freedom, the Mambises, led by Antonio Maceo, fortified themselves with the Daiquirí's parent, Canchánchara. It was simple blend of rum, lime juice and "honey": a term frequently used in Cuba in describe molasses. The drink was made in batches and poured into bottles. Strapped to their saddles, the bottled Canchánchara was not only a welcomed thirst-quencher for the freedom fighters during the long, arduous campaigns against the Spanish colonial army. It was also an excellent painkiller for the wounded.

The Canchánchara was certainly present twenty years later, at the height of the 1898 Spanish-American War when Daiquirí became the focal point of an offensive that saw Spanish troops attacked from the land by General Calixto García's Cuban Liberation Army and from the sea by Admiral William T Sampson's American naval forces led by General William Shafter, who landed 17,000 troops on the

OPPOSITE: From its birth as a refreshment for freedom fighters to its status as one of Ernest Hemingway's favorite drinks, the Daiquiri is a true Cuban classic.

shipping docks owned by the Spanish-American Iron Company on Daiquirí Bay.

Some Daiquirí legends say that when the 300-pound, 63-year-old Shafter first tasted the Canchánchara, he declared that "the only missing ingredient is ice."

COX & PAGLIUCHI

It is just prior to this epic moment that many authorities believe the Canchánchara evolved into the Daiquirí. New York mining engineer Jennings S. Cox, Jr. was the general manager of the Spanish-American Iron Company in 1896 and a member of the American Institute of Mining Engineers.

OPPOSITE:
The coasters
at El Floridita
proudly state the
establishment is the
cradle of the Daiquirí.

So was fellow engineer F.D. Pagliuchi, who later wrote an amazing account of the landing that was published in the 1898 *Harper's Pictorial History of the War with Spain*. He also photographed Liberation Army leaders Generals Juan Rius Rivera and Manual Ramón Silva. As an engineer, Pagliuchi conducted a great deal of published research into the mineral composition of Cuban mines and was likely consulting for Cox's company which had heavily invested in the region.

At the end of one day, Pagliuchi suggested it was cocktail time. Cox was out of gin and vermouth, the ingredients for a Martini. So Cox shook up rum, lime and sugar, possibly also inspired by the locals' consumption of Canchánchara.

Upon tasting it, Pagliuchi inquired, "What is this cocktail called?"

"It doesn't have a name, so it must be a Rum Sour," Cox replied.

"That's no name for such a fine, exquisite cocktail! We'll call it a Daiquirí!" Pagliuchi exclaimed.

LA CUNA DEL DAIQUIRÍ

After independence was won, the Daiquirí became a fashionable drink especially appreciated by mining engineers who frequented the Venus Hotel in Santiago de Cuba just to partake in this refreshment. It then made an appearance in Havana at the Plaza Hotel, introduced by its famed bartender Emilio González, who was more familiarly known as Maragato.

It was in the hands of Constantino Ribalaigua Vert, who took over La Florida in 1918, that the Daiquirí's children—the Hemingway Special and the Floridita Daiquirí—were born and thrived. Enthused by this simple sour concoction, Constante tested four versions. As United Press journalist Jack Cuddy documented in the 1937 book *Cock-*

tails: Bar la Florida, Constante tossed two ounces of rum into a cocktail shaker and then:

> *Add one teaspoon of finely granulated sugar. Do not use powdered sugar which Constantino insists has starch in it. Then add one teaspoon of Maraschino—a cordial which is made from wild cherries grown in Dalmatia. Squeeze the juice of half a lime. Next toss in finely shaved ice until the shaker is nearly full. This ice must be shaved so fine that it's almost snow. Do not use cracked ice. Then place the shaker under an electric mixer: one of those malted milk stirrers in American Drug stores. Let it stir for about three minutes. If you haven't an electric mixer, shake it rapidly in a regular cocktail shaker for about four minutes. Meanwhile chill your glasses by pouring in cracked ice and a bit of water. Now toss the cracked ice and water and strain your Daiquirí from the shaker into the glasses through a half-strainer—one that is not too fine.*

This frappéed version was an immediate hit. Technology helped Constante boost the number of Daiquirís he could produce by the late 1930s. That is when he ordered a Flak Mak ice-crushing machine from the United States. And when the Waring blender was launched in 1938, El Floridita was one of the first establishments to adopt its use behind the bar.

OPPOSITE:
The 1937 book
*Cocktails: Bar la
Florida* contained
numerous variations
on the classic
Daiquiri.

What was achieved with this new technological device was best documented by Ernest

Hemingway in his posthumously published 1970 novel *Islands in the Stream*:

> *He was drinking another frozen Daiquirí with no sugar in it and as he lifted it, heavy and the glass frost-rimmed, he looked at the clear part below the frapped top and it reminded him of the sea. The frapped part of the drink was like the wake of a ship and the clear part was the way the water looked when the bow cut it when you were in shallow water over marl bottom. That was almost the exact color.*

DAIQUIRÍ RECIPES

EL FLORIDITA'S DAIQUIRÍ is not limited to one or two. The drink evolved over the years in the hands of Constantino Ribalaigua Vert as seen in the 1937 *Cocktails: Bar la Florida*. It is interesting to note that recipes for this drink seem to have become much sweeter over the years.

The original Daiquirí No.1 as listed in *Cocktails: Bar la Florida* used one teaspoon of sugar to sweeten the juice of half a lime. More recently, recipes seem to call for more sugar syrup than lime juice.

Bar La Florida

Obispo y Monserrate
La Habana, Cuba

In general, the ratio between sour and sweet should be 2:1. This ratio changes however when making blended drinks because when super-chilled in a blender the relative perceived sweetness falls. A ratio of 1:1 is more appropriate to compensate.

A little extra dilution benefits the drink. This is achieved by shaking the cocktail on a combination of rock and a little crushed ice.

DAIQUIRÍ NO. 1

INGREDIENTS
60ml Havana Club Añejo 3 Años or Añejo Blanco
12.5ml Fresh squeezed lime juice
1 teaspoon Granulated sugar

METHOD
Shake the ingredients on a combination of crushed and rock ice and strain into a pre-chilled coupe glass. Garnish with a wedge of lime. If blending, double the amount of sugar and blend with approximately 10oz of crushed ice.

DAIQUIRÍ NO. 2 (VERSION A)

INGREDIENTS
60ml Havana Club Añejo 3 Años or Añejo Blanco
12.5ml Fresh squeezed lime juice
1 teaspoon Granulated sugar
10ml Fresh orange juice
5ml Curaçao

METHOD
Shake the ingredients on a combination of crushed and rock ice and strain into a pre-chilled coupe glass. Garnish with a twist

of orange. If blending, double the amount of curaçao and blend
with approximately 10oz of crushed ice.

DAIQUIRÍ NO. 2 (VERSION B)

This version is wonderful but obviously is only possible during the very short season for Seville Oranges.

INGREDIENTS
60ml Havana Club Añejo 3 Años or Añejo Blanco
20ml Fresh squeezed Seville orange juice
2 teaspoons Granulated sugar
10ml Curaçao

METHOD
Shake the ingredients on a combination of crushed and rock ice
and strain into a pre-chilled coupe glass. Garnish with a twist
of orange. If blending, double the amount of curaçao and blend
with approximately 10oz of crushed ice.

DAIQUIRÍ NO. 3 (B. ORBON)

INGREDIENTS
60ml Havana Club Añejo 3 Años or Añejo Blanco
10ml Fresh squeezed lime juice
5ml Fresh grapefruit juice
5ml Maraschino liqueur
1 teaspoon Granulated sugar

METHOD
Shake the ingredients on a combination of crushed and rock
ice and strain into a pre-chilled coupe glass. Garnish with a
wedge of lime and a cocktail cherry. If blending, double the
amount of sugar and maraschino liqueur before blending with

approximately 10oz of crushed ice.

DAIQUIRÍ NO. 4 (FLORIDITA DAIQUIRÍ)

INGREDIENTS
60ml Havana Club Añejo 3 Años or Añejo Blanco
12.5ml Fresh squeezed lime juice
5ml Maraschino liqueur
1 teaspoon Granulated sugar

METHOD
Shake the ingredients on a combination of crushed and rock ice
and strain into a pre-chilled coupe glass. Garnish with a wedge
of lime and a cocktail cherry. If blending, double the amount of
sugar and maraschino before blending with approximately 10oz
of crushed ice.

DAIQUIRÍ NO. 5

OPPOSITE:
Ernest Hemingway stayed
at the Hotel Ambos
Mundos when he first
encountered the Daiquirí.

INGREDIENTS
60ml Havana Club Añejo 3 Años or Añejo Blanco
12.5ml Fresh squeezed lime juice
5ml Homemade grenadine
(1 part fresh pomegranate juice to 2 parts sugar)
5ml Maraschino liqueur

METHOD
Shake the ingredients on a combination of crushed and rock ice
and strain into a pre-chilled coupe glass. Garnish with a wedge
of lime and a cocktail cherry. If blending, double the amount
of grenadine and maraschino liqueur before blending with
approximately 10oz of crushed ice.

Hemingway's Special

◇◇◇◇◇◇◇◇◇◇◇◇◇◇◇◇◇◇◇◇◇◇◇◇◇◇◇◇◇◇◇◇◇

RETURNING FROM THE HORRORS of the Spanish Civil War in 1938, Ernest Hemingway settled into room 511 at the Hotel Ambos Mundos on 153 Calle Obispo and began to write his novel *For Whom the Bell Tolls*. The story goes that Hemingway took a break one day and stopped into El Floridita at the other end of the street near Parque Central, where he ordered a Daiquirí from Constante.

OPPOSITE: Ernest Hemingway immortalized the cocktails at El Floridita and La Bodeguita del Medio with these simple lines which still hang over the bar at La Bodeguita del Medio.

In spite of the opinions of his doctor friends, Hemingway was convinced that he had diabetes. Consequently, he excluded all sugar from his diet, though he was never concerned about his alcohol consumption. Constante offered him a sugar-free Daiquirí with a double dose of Cuban rum. This Daiquirí Del Salvaje, soon became the Daiquirí a la Papa, then Daiquirí Como Papa.

Enamored with his new discovery, Hemingway returned every day at 11 AM dressed in Bermudas, short-sleeved shirt and espadrilles. He always sat on the same bar stool and downed a couple of his special Daiquirís. Sometimes he would return at 5 PM to consume a dozen more.

Later, *cantinero* Antonio Meilan modified the recipe by adding grapefruit juice and immortalized it under the appellation "Hemingway Special" or "Papa Doble".

After Hemingway moved out of the hotel and into his home La Finca Vigía, he continued

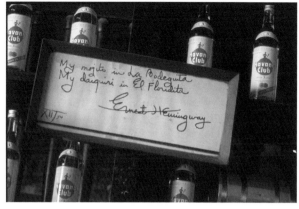

his frequent visits. Floridita's Daiquirís became such a source of inspiration for him that sometimes he brought in a thermos bottle to have it carefully filled with his favorite refreshment. Hemingway called this his *viaticum* [Latin for "provisions for a journey"], his *trago del camino* [gulp for the road], which helped him prolong the happy reverie begun in the Floridita during the ride back to La Finca Vigía in San Francisco de Paula.

HEMINGWAY SPECIAL (PAPA DOBLE)

INGREDIENTS
60ml Havana Club Añejo 3 Años or Añejo Blanco
15ml Fresh squeezed grapefruit juice
10ml Maraschino liqueur
5ml Fresh lime juice

METHOD
Shake the ingredients on a combination of crushed and rock ice and strain into a pre-chilled coupe glass. Garnish with a wedge of lime. If blending, double the amount of maraschino liqueur before blending with approximately 10oz of crushed ice.

Cuba Libre

◇◇◇◇◇◇◇◇◇◇◇◇◇◇◇◇◇◇

"CUBA LIBRE!" This was the battle cry of freedom-fighting Cubans from the days when the Mambises, led by Antonio Maceo, stormed the countryside during the Ten-Year War (1868-1878) and when the Cuban Liberation Army boldly fought the War of Independence (1895-1898) from Cienfuegos to Santiago, from Dos-Rios to Manzanillo.

No one is absolutely certain who invented this simple, refreshing concoction made with two of the world's most popular ingredients: Cuban rum and cola. Some people say it was invented in 1902 at La Florida to commemorate the island's independence.

A few facts substantiate part of this claim. According to the company's historical records, Coca-Cola was first exported in 1900 to Cuba, right after the very first bottle of syrup left the United States bound for Great Britain that very same year (Coca Cola had been invented only fourteen years earlier, in 1886 in Atlanta, Georgia). It is quite possible that glasses of rum and cola were served up icy cold to the celebrating politicians and diplomats who worked at the nearby Capitol Building.

CUBA LIBRE
INGREDIENTS
50ml Havana Club Añejo Especial or Reserva

½ Fresh lime
125ml Cola

METHOD
Muddle the half a lime in the bottom of a highball glass
before adding the rum. Then fill with rock ice and top with the
cola. Garnish with a wedge of lime. Muddling the lime is very
important as the bitter oils, as well as the juice, serve as a
counterpoint to the sweetness of the cola.

Made with an añejo, this drink is known as a Cubata.

More Cuban Classics

◇◇◇◇◇◇◇◇◇◇◇◇◇◇◇◇◇◇◇◇◇◇◇◇◇◇◇◇◇◇◇◇◇◇◇◇◇◇

MULATA

INVENTED BY Constante Ribalaigua Vert at La Florida, this
cocktail is essentially a chocolate-flavoured Daiquirí using
an older rum as the spirit base. It is usually a blended drink
so that is the recipe given below. If shaking the drink, do
not add the gomme syrup.

INGREDIENTS
50ml Havana Club Añejo 7 Años
12.5ml Fresh squeezed lime juice
15ml Dark crème de cacao
5ml Gomme syrup

METHOD
Blend the ingredients on 10oz of crushed ice before serving in a
coupe glass garnished with a lime wedge.

NACIONAL

THIS DRINK IS ALSO a Daiquirí or Rum Sour style of drink, but uses apricot brandy to add flavour and sweetness.

INGREDIENTS
50ml Havana Club Añejo Especial or Reserva
20ml Apricot brandy
12.5ml Fresh lime juice

METHOD
Shake all the ingredients on a combination of rock and crushed ice, then double strain into a chilled cocktail glass. Garnish with a wedge of lime.

SMALL- DINGER

THIS MARVELLOUS DRINK is the first cocktail listed in *Cocktails: Bar la Florida* and is a great example of a drink that successful refutes the notion that only one spirit base should be used in a cocktail. Here the addition of gin to the rum gives this sour-style drink a herbaceous complexity.

INGREDIENTS
25ml Havana Club Añejo 3 Años or Añejo Blanco
25ml Beefeater Gin
12.5ml Fresh lime juice
10ml Homemade grenadine (see Daiquirí No. 5 for recipe)

METHOD
Shake all the ingredients on a combination of rock and crushed ice. Then double strain into a chilled cocktail glass and garnish with pomegranate seeds and a wedge of lime.

MARY PICKFORD

THIS ENIGMATIC DRINK, made especially for the silent-screen star Mary Pickford by Constante Ribalaigua Vert, appears on paper to be far too sweet and only works when freshly squeezed pineapple juice is used or muddled fresh pineapple chunks. On no account use sweetened juice. Likewise the maraschino liqueur should be the dry style. However when all the ingredients are correct this drink is a marvel.

INGREDIENTS
50ml Havana Club Añejo 3 Años or Añejo Blanco
10ml Maraschino liqueur
5ml Homemade grenadine (see Daiquirí No. 5 for recipe)
Whole 1.5cm slice of fresh pineapple (chopped with the skin removed)

METHOD
Muddle the pineapple pieces with the grenadine and maraschino. Add the rum and shake on a combination of rock and crushed ice. Then double strain into a cocktail glass and garnish with a twist of orange and a wedge of pineapple.

EL PRESIDENTE

STRANGELY, for a Manhattan style drink this recipe works better when shaken. The original recipes called for Chambéry Dry Vermouth but this makes too dry a cocktail, hence substituting Lillet Blanc.

INGREDIENTS
50ml Havana Club Añejo Especial or Reserva
25ml Lillet Blanc
10ml Curaçao

METHOD
Shake all the ingredients on rock ice and double strain into a
chilled cocktail glass. Garnish with a twist of orange and a
cherry.

CHAPARRA

THIS RECIPE comes from the 1937 *Cocktails: Bar la Florida*
and closely resembles an El Presidente, however its citrus
notes come from a spiral of lime zest and sweet vermouth
is used rather than dry.

INGREDIENTS
50ml Havana Club Añejo 3 Años or Añejo Blanco
25ml Noilly Prat Rouge
½ teaspoon Granulated sugar
1 zest Whole lime

METHOD
Dissolve the sugar using the vermouth in a mixing glass, before
adding the rum and rock ice. Then stir to chill. Take a chilled
cocktail glass and aromatize with the spiral zest of a whole
lime. Then strain the cocktail into the glass and garnish with the
whole lime zest.

RUM DAISY

THIS RECIPE is similar to the Mojito above in that the cocktail is aromatized with sprigs of mint, as well as Yellow Chartreuse and Angostura Bitters. It is adapted from the recipe in the 1937 *Cocktails: Bar La Florida.*

INGREDIENTS
50ml Havana Club Añejo 3 Años or Añejo Blanco
12.5ml Fresh lime juice (also zest of ½ lime)
1 teaspoon Granulated sugar
1 dash Angostura Bitters
10ml Yellow Chartreuse
2 stalks Fresh mint

METHOD
Aromatize a highball glass with the zest of half a lime. Then add the sugar, Angostura, lime juice and mint. Stir to dissolve the sugar and extract the mint oils. Add the rum and fill the glass with crushed ice. Gently churn to mint. Top with more crushed ice and add a float of the Yellow Chartreuse. Garnish with mint sprigs, a cherry and seasonal fruits.

And Who Drank Them

THIS PARTICULAR LITERARY CONSECRATION may be a little hasty, though wittily formulated. A version of it was inscribed by a nervous hand above the signature of "Adriano" on one of the multicolored walls of La Bodeguita del Medio:

> *I've drunk a lot of Mojitos, just like Ernest Hemingway, I've slept and I've woken up and I haven't*

*got any Nobel Prize (cheer up, me neither). But
I'm happy...*

And why not? The last thing Adriano would have
seen before dozing off would have been the faces of Brigitte
Bardot and Sophia Loren, pinned up on Bodeguita's "wall of
fame". Yes, they were here, too. They sat at the same ABOVE:
Ernest Hemingway
with Spencer Tracy at
El Floridita.
tables as Hemingway, Rocky Marciano, Gary Cooper,
Errol Flynn, Spencer Tracy, Marlene Dietrich, Luis
Miguel Dominguin, Frank Sinatra, Ava Gardner, Rita
Hayworth and dozens more enchanted by Cuba and its tropi-
cal *joie de vivre*. They followed in the footsteps of their illus-
trious predecessors—Greta Garbo, Mary Pickford, Douglas
Fairbanks—and even drank the cocktails that were made by
Havana's finest *cantineros* in their honour.

Lights, camera, action. Hollywood seemed to have
erected a movie set at the corner of Calle Monserrate and
Calle Obispo. El Floridita welcomed motion picture idols as
well as the cream of the crop from Miami, New York and
Paris. As special correspondent of the on-going Havana

party, author Fernando Campoamor had a box seat and a mandate: He wouldn't be forgiven if he was outdone on his home turf by American gossip columnist Louella Parsons or *Screenland* magazine's Linda Carter.

How could he know where to be when so many bold-faced names would show up without notice at the Hotel Nacional, at the Riviera, or at the Sevilla? Fernando had his lookouts, spies and informers scouring every prime spot. His diligence paid off. He managed to interview Errol Flynn and get a first-hand report from a police-buddy on George Raft's turbulent night at the Capri. And there was one person who always walked straight into his net: Nat King Cole.

"He was my only real friend. He was worshipped here, as if he'd been born in Havana. He was more Cuban than me. When he performed at the Tropicana, the house was sold out in an hour. The jet set poured in, actors came specially from the States, the biggest gangsters, from Naples, New York and Miami, as well as from Havana too. We had a gentlemen's agreement, Nat and me. Every time he came here, at the end of the show at the Marianao, I came and picked him up and we went home," Campoamor fondly recalled.

The beauty of the Cuban palette is that it blends bold with soft, defined and misty. The combinations are endless and distinctively Cuban color.

CHAPTER SEVEN

Cuban Color

CUBAN RUM & CUBAN CULTURE

IN THE PROLOGUE to his second book of poems *Motivos de Son*, Nicolás Guillén proudly proclaimed in his prologue: "The spirit of Cuba is mestizo. And from the spirit to the skin the definitive color comes to us. Some day they will say: 'Cuban color.'"

EVERY PERSON WHO HAS VISITED and fallen in love with Cuba has read and understood Guillén's words. A place like none other, the textures and depth created by the marriage of Spanish and African cultures with sprinklings of other influences make Cuba a uniquely inspiring world unto itself. Whether Cubans descend from indigenous Caribbeans; Spanish, British, or French colonists; African slaves; indentured Chinese workers,

BELOW:
Descended from a broad spectrum of ethnicities, Cubans are a remarkably diverse blend unlike any other.

Arabs, North Americans and complete South American Diaspora, they have added brilliantly-coloured threads to the island's lush cultural fabric.

In fact, it is this exuberant mix blended
with its tropical environs that has created
a remarkable land filled with tenderness, love,
passion, fury and a love for rich history.

Cuba's tropical breezes, its beaches, its streets, its bars, its restaurants and its people have always roused the hearts and minds of writers and artists from far-off lands. Many found a reason to visit more than once. Some lingered on to savor the island's atmosphere. One thing they all had in common: each told the story of this enchanted island from a wholly unique perspective.

British novelist Graham Greene visited Cuba nearly a dozen times in the 1950s and 1960s, always stayed at the Hotel Nacional and always ordering an *añejo* rum at the bar, which he said tasted like "ship's wood, like a sea voyage." (Anyone who has reclined on the deck of a teak sailboat in the afternoon sunshine will immediately understand his description.) He closely befriended Cuban novelist-journalist Lisandro Otero, poet-essayist Pablo Armando Fernandez and poet-playwright Virgilio Piñera.

Otero recounted in his memoirs, *Llove Sobre Mojado*, that in 1957, Greene was determined to trek up into the Sierra Maestra Mountains and interview Fidel Castro. Despite making contacts in Santiago de Cuba with people who could aid him in his quest, his ascent to the mountains and meeting with Castro were postponed. Greene finally got his wish during his last two visits to Cuba in the 1960s when he had the opportunity to spend hours in Castro's company. According to Greene, it was a moment he savored for the rest of his days.

The Cuban spirit and Cuban rum has fueled and inspired internationally-renowned writers from Greene and Hemingway, to Jean-Paul Sartre and Federico Garcia Lorca, to Miguel Ángel Asturias and Gabriel Garciá Marquez.

That influence also led to the success of musical greats such as Nat King Cole, who went to Havana in 1958 to record the first of three highly popular albums he performed entirely in Spanish with the help of musician-arranger Armando Romeu. What was the sound that captured Cole's soul? He heard it sung by the *trovadores* as he sipped Mojitos and Daiquirís. It was the sound of Cuba, the sound of *son cubano*.

Son Cubano

<><><><><><><><><><><><><><><><>

MUSIC IS HEARD throughout the day, throughout the night in Havana, in Santiago de Cuba, in the countryside. Writer Fernando Ortiz Fernández once described Cuban music as "auditory rum entering the ears and all the senses with a special effect of rallying and uniting people and energizing day-to-day life." Taking inspiration from Africa, Spain and the Caribbean, *son cubano* is the sound that bore children the world craves to feel: rumba, cha-cha, salsa.

Its ancestor *changüí* was born in the early 1800s in Guantánamo, amid the sugarcane mills and surrounding rural slave communities. Men danced to *changüí* to display their chivalry accompanied by the percussive rhythms of the marimbula and bongos, sounds that originated with the Bantu and Arara tribes of Africa. Women swayed flirtatiously to *changüí,* guided by the lyrical *tres* [3x2-stringed guitar] and *gûiro.* Evoking the spirit of Spanish *boleros*, accompanying singers recounted the joys and sorrows of love.

OPPOSITE:
A Cuban *changüí* band posed for this photograph which was taken in the late 1800s.

From this lush parentage, *el son* was born in the late 1800s in Baracoa in Guantánamo province. Musicologist Helio Orovio documented that in 1892, Nene Manfugás brought the *tres* and the melodic voice of *el son* from its birthplace to Santiago de Cuba. Around 1910, the sound reached Havana

and was recorded within the decade by the groups Sexteto Habanero and Sexteto Boloña. The arrival of radio to Cuba, in 1922, gave *son cubano* its wings, spreading it across the island.

Roving *trovadores* such as José Chicho Ibánez, Rosendo Ruiz, Manuel Corona and Santiago-born Sindo Garay carried *son cubano* through the streets of Old Havana. As he recounted of his early days: "At nightfall, I would take my guitar and seek my *trovador* friends. All night long we would stroll Havana's perfumed gardens, stopping to serenade mysterious señoritas behind grill work windows. At La Bodeguita, we would nurse our inspiration on Cancháncharas, a drink with honey, spices and fragrant rum. What a delight!"

OPPOSITE: Sindo Garay was one of Havana's most revered *trovadores* and composer of the song "Mujer Bayamesa".

Author Federico Garcia Lorca once called Garay "Cuba's Great Pharoah". With his deeply-lined face and deep-set eyes, the diminutive Garay serenaded the world from party to party, *bodega* to *bodega*. Before life began to etch its long story on the diminutive Garay's face, he was so inspired by the beauty of sunrise over the town of Bayamo, in 1918, he wrote a song that best portrays the beauty of his musical gift, *Mujer Bayamesa*:

> *Lleva en su alma la bayamesa*
> *tristes recuerdos de tradiciones*
> *cuando contempla sus verdes llanos*

lá/grimas vierte por sus pasiones.

Ella es sencilla, le brinda al hombre
virtudes todas y el corazon

Pero si siente de la Patria el grito, (BIS)
todo lo deja, todo lo quema,
ese es su lema, su religin.

[TRANSLATION]
In her soul, the Bayamo woman carries
sad memories of old traditions
When she looks at her green pastures
tears well up in her eyes

She is simple, she offers mankind
all virtues and her heart

But if she hears her homeland's cry
she drops everything, she burns everything
That is her life, her religion.

American tourism to Cuba during the Prohibition era influenced the next musical evolution—*mambo*. Mixing European social dance music with the rhythms of African folk compositions, in 1938, Orestes and Cachao López wrote and performed a piece called *Mambo*. Dance steps were crafted around its new music genre five years later by musician Perez Prado, who introduced the new moves and sounds at Havana's La Tropicana nightclub.

OPPOSITE:
Perez Prado introduced to world to the *mambo* dance steps at La Tropicana nightclub in Havana.

ABOVE:
Enrique Jorrín pioneered the *cha-cha-chá*, marrying *son cubano* and *mambo*.

Mambo went mainstream and moved to the United States. Born in Catalonia and raised in Havana, singer-songwriter Xavier Cugat imported *mambo* to New York, when he became resident band leader of the Waldorf-Astoria hotel's orchestra. One of his most popular mambo recordings was rose to the top of the American charts when it was covered by the Andrews Sisters during the Second World War: "Rum and Coca Cola."

Helio Orovio attributes the birth of *cha-cha-chá* to a single composer, Enrique Jorrín, who in 1948, married the lyrical style of *son cubano* with the dance-oriented pace of *mambo*.

Journalist Israel Sanchez-Coll commented that "What Jorrín composed, by his own admission, were nothing but creatively modified *danzones*."

The well-known name came into being with the help of the dancers [of the Silver Star Club in Havana], when, in inventing the dance that was coupled to the rhythm, it was discovered that their feet were making a peculiar sound as they grazed the floor on three successive beats: *cha-cha-chá* and from this sound was born, by onomatopoeia, the name that caused people all around the world to want to move their feet."

Cuba's musical spirit cast an even wider net during the 1960s and 1970s, spreading throughout the Caribbean and Latin America with the development of *salsa*. Incorporating *cha-cha-chá* and *son cubano*, the music was born from Cuban and Puerto Rican emigrés who settled in New York, adding pop, jazz and rock instruments and elements. Driven to popularity by music greats such as Tito Puente, Machito and Panamanian-born Rubén Blades, *salsa* has become an icon of Latin American culture. The sound of clicking glasses of icy-cold Mojitos, Daiquirís, Piña Coladas and Cuba Libres punctuate the salsa rhythms felt on dance floors in Havana, New York, London, Paris, Berlin and even Tokyo.

BELOW: Singer Celia Cruz was a major ambassador of *salsa* throughout the world.

But as *salsa* singer Celia Cruz once commented to world-music historian Sue Steward, "Salsa is Cuban music with another name. It's *mambo, cha-cha-chá, rumba, son*...all the Cuban rhythms under one name."

OPPOSITE:
Embracing both
shamanistic and Christian
beliefs, this *santería* altar
exemplifies the many ways
Cubans have adopted and
assimilated numerous
cultures.

Since the 1990s, Cuban music has experienced a revival throughout the world. The international success of the Buena Vista Social Club, Compay Segundo, Ibrahim Ferrer and Omara Portuondo has sparked a rediscovery and appreciation of *son cubano*. Cuban *salsa* has once again evolved and is heard through the sounds and voices of Los Van Van, NG La Banda, Paulito FG and Charanga Habanera.

Journalist for Britain's *The Guardian* newspaper Gavin McOwen commented in a 2004 article that "music is a religion in Havana." Just like its music, Cuba's spiritual nature is crafted from Spanish Roman Catholic, indigenous Caribbean and Yoruban shamanistic traditions. It goes by a special name, *santería*.

Honouring the Saints

A RITUAL TAKES PLACE EVERY DAY throughout Cuba. Whether it is in a bar, a restaurant, at home, or on the beach, when a fresh bottle of rum is opened the first drop of rum is allowed to fall to the ground. A true Cuban will do that anywhere in the world: the place makes no difference. And Cubans introduce this ritual to all who visit.

"This is our passport", said Trinidad architect Macholo with a humorous note. "We get a lot of applications for naturalization. When my friends spend a few days at the house, whether they're French, Italians, or Spaniards, they also sanctify the floor with a drop of rum and then another because it's their last day in Trinidad."

This spilling of rum stems from a *santería* ritual performed by its believers who revere the Yoruban deity Changó, the Sky Father, the god of drums, thunder and lightning, a master dancer and drummer. Changó embodies passion, virility and power.

"Without rum I cannot worship Changó, you see. And if I don't honor my saint at least once a month I will be damned. I need Changó just as much as I need the rising sun each day," a Havana resident named Angelito confessed. He spills a drop to sanctify the ground before a small altar to the deity that rests in a corner of his room. Then he takes a sip from the bottle, which is how it is prescribed to "give rum to the saint."

Some people say it is because all Cuban men are sons of Changó (the god who loves all women) that they know a thousand ways to tell a woman she is beautiful. Not surprisingly his Catholic counterpart is Saint Barbara, a patron who guards against lightning and protects those who work with explosives. One story explains the association: Changó had to dress as a woman to flee from an enemy who intended to kill him. Maybe that is why Changó is frequently invoked and revered because communion with this deity helps one overcome powerful enemies.

Cut to another scene, a *toque de santos* [saints' touch]. Angelito is there, at the apartment of a *santeró* [priest] who is garbed in blue and gold robes. More than a dozen white-clad worshippers have gathered. Those who are asking for his protection have donned red-beaded necklaces. On an altar there is a *batea*, representing the royal palm in which Changó resides. Offerings of plantains, cooked okra, cornmeal with palm oil, are placed there for him to eat. The aromas of Jericho rose, cedar wood and sarsaparilla waft from a metal bowl.

**Each worshipper pours out
an offering of rum onto the damp floor.**

Once the deity has consumed his meal, a revelry begins. Drums play in the background, played by white-clad musicians, while the congregation sway to the mesmerizing rhythm. If they are fortunate, one of the assembled with receive Changó's spirit: the deity will speak to some of them, bless them with a touch to the forehead, will take a sip of rum and spray it on their feet, protecting them from harm and filling them with passionate love.

La Giraldilla

THIS LEGEND OF CUBA ends with a story about love: the enduring love of a woman who still waits and watches for the return of her husband. High atop the Castillo de la Real Fuerza, the former governor's residence, she looks out over Havana harbour, hoping the next ship on the horizon will bear the man of her heart back into her arms.

The story is about conquistador Hernando de Soto and his beautiful wife, Doña Isabel de Bobadilla, daughter of the founder of Panama City, Pedro Arias Dávila. Already famous for his role in the 1530 conquest of the Incan Empire, de Soto married Isabel upon his return to Spain. On 20 March 1537, King Carlos I of Spain granted de Soto the governorship of Cuba and ordered him to colonize North America within four years.

Inspired by returning explorer Cabeza de Vaca's tales of gold and riches and Ponce de Leon's expeditions in Florida, De Soto selected 620 eager young Spanish and Portuguese volunteers to help him defend Cuba against marauding corsairs and pirates as well as conquer North

America in the name of the Spanish crown. Isabel joined her husband and his men, voyaging far from home to be with her husband, whom she passionately loved.

Two years later, de Soto and his men embarked from Havana, hopeful that riches and glory would greet them upon their return. De Soto appointed Isabel as governor—the only woman to ever take the role. From that day on, the legend says, she spent long hours in the castle's surveillance tower, hoping for and anxiously awaiting her husband's safe return.

De Soto never returned to Havana harbour. After leading his men from the Florida peninsula westward, he died of fever, in 1542, while exploring the western banks of the Mississippi River, still in search of gold and glory. It is said that when she finally received news of her husband's death, Doña Isabel herself died of a broken heart.

The passionate love Isabel displayed for her husband inspired Havana sculptor Gerónimo Martin Pínzon, in 1634, to create La Giraldilla: a symbol of true love, of marital fidelity and of eternal hope. Governor Don Juan Bitrián Viamonte ordered the sculpture to be cast in brass and placed as a weather vane atop the castle's surveillance tower. Governor Bitrián then named the statue La Giraldilla, after a figure by the same name that stands stop the Giralda Cathedral in his native city of Seville, Spain.

Today, La Giraldilla is the symbol of both the city of Havana and of Havana Club rum, watching the horizon while holding the Cross of Calatrava in her right hand. She is a symbol of an eternal romance between Cuba and its remarkable people; between its people and their love of life itself.

Select Bibliography

Bonera, Miguel. *Oro Blanco: Una Historia Empresarial del Ron Cubano, Tomo I.* Toronto: Lugus Libros Latinamerica Inc., 2000.

Brown, Jared and Miller, Anistatia. "Pivotal Figures: Johann Tobias Lowitz". Berlin: Mixology Magazin, 2008.

Brown, Jared and Miller, Anistatia. *The Soul of Brasil.* London: Mixellany Books, 2008.

Campoamor, Fernando G. *El Hijo Alegre de la Caña de Azúcar.* La Habana: Instituto Cubano del Libro Editorial científico-Técnica, 1985

Casas, Bartolomé de las. *Brevísima relación de la destrucción de las Indias.* London : Printed for R. Hewson, 1689.

Cocktails: Bar La Florida. La Habana: La Florida, 1937.

Cordier, Henri and Yule, Henry, translator and editor. *The Book of Ser Marco Polo, the Venetian : concerning the kingdoms and marvels of the East.* Third edition. London : J. Murray, 1903.

Diderot, Denis and d'Alember, Jean Lerond. *Encyclopédie, ou, Dictionnaire raisonné des sciences, des arts et des métiers, par une société de gens de letters.* Paris: Le Breton, 1751-1765.

"Escapes from Bandits". New York: *The New York Times*, 14 October 1911.

Hale, Edward Everett. *The life of Christopher Columbus : from his own letters and journals and other documents of his time.* Chicago : G.L. Howe, 1891.

Lam, Rafael. *The Bodeguita del Medio.* La Habana: Editorial José Martí, 1994.

"Obituary: Jennings S Cox Jr." New York: *The New York Times*, 2 September 1913.

"Obituary: Jennings S Cox". New York: *The New York Times*, 22 October 1913.

"Our Landing in Cuba". New York: *The New York Times*, 10 July 1898.

Pagliuchi, F.D. "How a Filibustering Expedition Was Landed". *Harper's Pictorial History of the War with Spain*. New York: Harper & Brothers, Publishers, 1898.

Pequena Historia del Bar Boadas. Barcelona: Gráficas Vila SA, 1993.

Skeat, Walter W. English *Etymology: Chiefly Reprinted from the Transactions of the Philological Society*. Oxford: Clarendon Press, 1901.

Sloppy Joe's Cocktail Manual. La Habana: Sloppy Joe's, 1936.

Smith, Frederick H. *Caribbean Rum: A Social and Eocnomic History*. Gainesville: University Press of Florida, 2005.

Steward, Sue. *Salsa: Musical heartbeat of Latin America*. London: Thames & Hudson Ltd, 1999.

Travel Magazine. Florida Park NY, 1922.

CPSIA information can be obtained
at www.ICGtesting.com
Printed in the USA
2638LVUK00001B